GOSPEL CHARACTERS

By the same author:

Published by Hodder and Stoughton:

THE NEED TO PREACH

Published by Hodder and Stoughton, Harpers and the Ryerson Press;

BARRIERS TO CHRISTIAN BELIEF
THE ETERNAL LEGACY
THE CRUCIAL ENCOUNTER

Published by Hodder and Stoughton and Word Inc. :

GOD IN MAN'S EXPERIENCE
ILLUSIONS OF OUR CULTURE

Published by the Lutterworth Press, the Abingdon Press and the Ryerson Press;

GOD AND HIS PEOPLE
THE ROMAN LETTER TODAY
BENEATH THE CROSS OF JESUS
WHAT IS A CHRISTIAN?
GOD'S TIME AND OURS
THIS IS LIVING

Published by the Independent Press and the Abingdon Press:

PATHWAYS TO HAPPINESS

Published by the Epworth Press:

A PILGRIMAGE TO THE HOLY LAND

Published by Word Inc.

WE HAVE THIS MINISTRY
EPHESIANS: A POSITIVE AFFIRMATION

Published by the Upper Room

HANG ON TO THE LORD'S PRAYER

GOSPEL CHARACTERS

The Personalities Around Jesus

by

Leonard Griffith

WILLIAM B. EERDMANS PUBLISHING COMPANY
Grand Rapids, Michigan

DEDICATED

WITH

UNDYING GRATITUDE AND LOVE

TO THE MEMORY OF

MY PARENTS

Library of Congress Cataloging in Publication Data

Griffith, Arthur Leonard, 1920–
    Gospel characters.

    1. Jesus Christ—Friends and associates.   2. Bible.
N.T.   Gospels—Biography.   I. Title.
BS2430.G74   1976   225.9'22 [B]   76–12412
ISBN 0–8028–1646–0

Contents

Introduction

Every book has to begin somewhere. This one began in a Toronto dining room where I was having lunch with Edward England, Religious Editor of Hodder and Stoughton. He suggested that the time was ripe for someone to write a series of volumes on Bible characters in the tradition of the classic and comprehensive series written by Alexander Whyte of Edinburgh more than half a century ago.

Not that a modern writer may be expected to improve on the work done by Dr. Whyte. His series are not out of date but they are out of print, they have become collector's items. They can be found only in theological libraries or on the shelves of second-hand book shops.   Mr. England believed that the reading public might welcome a new series presented in the idiom and clothed in the symbols of our modern day. They would be shorter and less exhaustive and might comprise three volumes, the first from the Gospels, the second from the Acts and Epistles, the third from the Old Testament.

When Mr. England invited me to consider the project, I responded with immediate enthusiasm. History, especially sacred history, is not only a chronicle of events but a story of people and the way they reacted to those events. The people in the Bible have always fascinated me. I have lived with them for many years and feel that I know some of them not as ancient characters but as living personalities in whom we can see ourselves.

Right away that raises the problem of selection. Obviously some characters are more important and interesting than others. Whom to include in the limited space of this book and whom to leave out? The amount or scarcity of information cannot be the sole criterion. We might know several facts about a person, none of which really provide the clue to his character. We might know only one fact about another person, something he did or said, that really lets us see inside him and shows us the kind of person he was. Studying the first four books of the New Testament in preparation for this volume, I realised that basically they are a biography of one person, Jesus of Nazareth, and that the relative significance of other persons depends on the way they interacted with him.

Several times in the ensuing chapters I have used the theatrical metaphor, seeing the Gospel story as a great drama of redemption with Jesus as the principal figure on the stage. He is surrounded by a large cast of supporting characters, some of whom actually do support him while others try to knock him down. I finally grouped them into the categories of those who prepared his way, those who followed him, those who were helped by him, those who opposed him, and those who saw him die.

At least two of the categories could be expanded and made the subject of separate full-length volumes. Many excellent books have been written about the twelve disciples who followed Jesus. In keeping with the scheme of this book I have settled upon four — Peter, John, Matthew and Thomas — whose lives Jesus changed or affected most profoundly. Judas Iscariot belongs in the category of those who opposed Jesus. Many of the people who were helped by the personal ministry of Jesus appear in the pages of my own earlier book, *The Crucial Encounter*; and, not wanting to repeat myself, I have omitted them from this volume. That explains the exclusion of prominent character such as Nicodemus and Zaccheus and the Penitent Thief. It explains the inclusion of relatively obscure characters such as the Canaanite Woman and the Roman Centurion.

For me it was a challenging and rewarding exercise not only to learn about the people who surrounded Jesus when he was on earth but to learn from them and discover where we relate to them in their relation to Jesus. In some cases I have done little more than collate the abundant Bible material; in other cases I have drawn freely on the commentaries, the encyclopaedias and my own imagination. I have used different vehicles of presentation, among them the dialogue, the imaginary interview, the dramatic soliloquy and the sermon.

Except where otherwise indicated, I have quoted consistently from the text of the New English Bible. I have carefully footnoted my sources of information, though I am left with a sense of unexpressed indebtedness to many writers of similar volumes whose insights I have assimilated and unconsciously used. (My thanks are due to Mrs. Isabelle Macklin who typed the manuscript and the proof reader.)

Leonard Griffith

Toronto, 1975.

1. Published by Oliphant, Anderson and Ferrier, Edinburgh and London.
2. There is a comparatively recent two-volume edition in the Zondervan Reprint Classics: *Whyte's Bible Characters* (Zondervan Publishing House, Grand Rapids, Michigan, 1952).
3. Published by Hodder and Stoughton, London, 1965.

I

These Prepared His Way

1
Mary

The Best Supporting Character

THE CURTAIN IS about to rise on the greatest drama ever played on the stage of history. There is only one star in that drama — Jesus Christ, the Star of all worlds, all times and all souls. But it's not a one-man show. There is a large cast of supporting characters, some who play major roles, others who play bit parts. All perform brilliantly. All deserve recognition. Which one shall we single out for an award as the *best* supporting character?

If we listen to our hearts we shall probably choose Mary, the mother of Jesus, and we shall be backed up in our choice by Luke, the author of the third Gospel. In his opening chapters, that tell of Jesus' birth, Mary stands continually in the centre of the stage. Luke takes her out of her niche in the wall, brings her to life and makes her a real person in the Redemption Drama.

In the life of any man his mother is usually the best supporting character. She is the person to whom he must always say, "If it weren't for you, I should not be here." That is true in a biological sense, true also in a larger sense. Many a man at the pinnacle of success has said to his mother, "If it weren't for you, I should not be here." Abraham Lincoln was not the first or the last man to say, "All that I am and all that I have I owe to my mother."

Too rarely does a mother receive the recognition she deserves. Occasionally it does happen, and then our hearts are strangely warmed. A few years ago an American university honoured the name of Niebuhr — not the late Reinhold

Niebuhr, a scholar so versatile that the President of Harvard University offered to make him the professor of any chair of which he chose to be professor. Nor his brother, Richard Niebuhr, nor their sister Hulda Niebuhr, who also were bright stars in the theological firmament. The award in the form of an honorary degree went to the best supporting character in this brilliant cast, the one without whom the drama could not have been played at all — their aged mother.

We can applaud that award without being sentimental. A man's mother is not only a supporting character, she is *the* supporting character. She bears him in her body, ushers him into the world and feeds him at her breast, she makes a home for him and brings him up, she gives him goals, teaches him ideals and fires his ambitions, she loves him, helps him, suffers with him and stands by him when all others have forsaken him. There is more than sentiment in these tender lines of Rudyard Kipling,

> If I were hanged on the highest hill,
>   Mother o'mine, O mother o'mine!
> I know whose love would follow me still,
>   Mother o'mine, O mother o'mine!

Jesus was hanged on the highest hill, hanged like a common criminal before the hateful gaze of the whole world. His mother's love followed him there. At the close of the Gospel story we find Mary suffering with her son on Calvary. That is not unusual in a mother's experience. Whatever else motherhood means, it means suffering. Mary suffered with Jesus from the very beginning.

The Wondrous Birth

Her suffering began even before he was born. It raises the inevitable question — Was Mary really a virgin, as the New Testament suggests and as some Catholic and Protestant traditions insist that she was? At the risk of evading the question, though not minimising its importance, we shall take the Gospel story at its face value.

Here is the lovely and innocent Mary, a girl not yet out of her teens, in the first blush of betrothal. She and Joseph, the carpenter of Nazareth, have just become engaged to be married. A busy and exciting time lies ahead of them as they make preparations for their wedding. One day, on her way home from the village well, Mary sets down the water pot and stops to rest for a moment, her thoughts lost in happy anticipation. Suddenly a blinding light envelops her, and as her eyes become accustomed to it, she sees an angelic presence and hears a voice that sounds like nothing on earth saying to her, "Greetings, most favoured one! The Lord is with you." Mary falls to her knees in fear. "Do not be afraid, Mary," says the angel, "for God has been gracious to you." Then follows the unbelievable news that of all the maidens who ever lived she has been divinely chosen to be the mother of the child who will grow up to be the world's Saviour. But is it such a favour? Is it even possible? Falteringly Mary answers the angel, "How can this be? I am still a virgin." "The Holy Spirit will come upon you," replies the angel.[1] A miraculous favour indeed, but try explaining it to the townspeople when they saw the first signs of her pregnancy. They dealt harshly with an unmarried mother. Try explaining it to Joseph who believed her to be as pure as the driven snow.

We can appreciate why large segments of the Christian world have made a special place in heaven for Mary the Mother of Jesus. Consider what God asked of this unsullied and unprotected girl and consider the simplicity of her response: "I am the Lord's servant; as you have spoken, so be it."[2] Mary was saying, "Yes, I accept all the shame, all the disgrace and all the possible suffering that this pregnancy involves, if that is the part I am to play in God's redemptive plan." Doesn't that make Mary of all women the most to be honoured? We may not idolise her or say our prayers to her but we do honour her as the one who shows us the way of perfect obedience to the will of God. Someone has said that the Incarnation began when Mary said, "Into thy hands I commend my body," and ended when Jesus said, "Into thy hands I commend my spirit."

Meanwhile, what of Joseph, whose whole world must have collapsed when Mary confessed her secret to him? He did not expose her publicly, as some men might have done, but he did break the engagement and perhaps Mary's heart. And Mary herself? What could she do? Where could she go? It is suggested that she may have been an orphan, and that is why she immediately travelled south to Hebron to visit her aged relative, Elizabeth, who also was expecting a child and who may have been a true mother to Mary in her need. It is suggested also that Joseph, after God revealed to him the truth about Mary's pregnancy, followed her to Hebron and brought her back to his home in Nazareth. Was that when Mary sang the Magnificat, telling forth the great things that God had done for her and the great things that he would do through her wondrous Son?[3]

How Mary must have suffered at the birth of Jesus! It coulldn't have come at a worse time. No woman in the last week of pregnancy should travel anywhere, let alone make a journey of six days over rough roads on the back of a donkey. Mary had no choice if she wanted to be with Joseph in Bethlehem, the place where he had to go to be registered by order of the Roman government. At Bethlehem there was no room in the inn, no lodging in any house, no shelter from the chill night air, no place to lie down but a stable where animals bedded in the straw. There in that lowliest of all places Mary, without the aid of a physician or midwife, brought the little life from the warmth and security of her body into the cold and perilous world of men. He belonged to her before he belonged to us, and it was she who gave him to us. Yet there was some comfort for Mary that night — a visit from shepherds who told of a strange sight on the Judean hills and a strange announcement from God. Mary "treasured up all these things and pondered over them."[4] Like every true mother she made a photograph album in her heart.

Mother and Son

A christening is usually a happy occasion. It should have been a time of great joy for the Holy Family when Mary and Joseph presented their child to God in the temple and especially when the aged Simeon took the infant in his arms and recognised him as the Saviour of Israel. Every mother's heart swells with pride when great things are prophesied for her child; but what if a sword also is prophesied, a sword that shall pierce the mother's heart?[5]

That sword struck soon and would have destroyed the Holy Family but for the protecting power of God. Under cover of night they fled to Egypt where they remained as refugees until they heard that the murderous King Herod was dead.[6] Then they went home to Nazareth for a period of years that are a closed book to us. They must have been happy years, especially for the child growing up in a loving home. In Nazareth today women still draw water from the well known as Mary's Well. As you see a mother coming away from it, bearing her water pot and followed by a little lad, you think of the boy Jesus clutching his mother's skirts, looking up into her face with trusting eyes and asking her the very questions that one day the whole world would ask him. Of those silent years the Gospel tells us only that "the child grew big and stong and full of wisdom; and God's favour was upon him."[7] That speaks of a mother's love and influence.

As a boy Jesus must have been unusually interested in religion, and his mother must surely have encouraged that interest. Memories of my own mother help me to understand and appreciate what that means. In my boyhood I had an unusual interest in religion. On Sunday mornings I sang in the choir of an Anglican church, and on Sunday evenings I conducted a service in our own living room. The furniture was rearranged in the style of a chancel to include an altar, a lectern and a pulpit, and I moved from one to the other just like a professional. My mother played the hymns on an old-fashioned pump organ. She was organist, choir and congregation. I came through the door wearing one of her black dresses with a white shirt on top and a red scarf hung around my neck. I was a processional of one except for the household cat. Then I opened the Prayer Book and read Evensong, my mother providing the responses. I even preached a sermon to her. She didn't laugh at her eccentric son but "treasured up all these things in her heart."[8] More photographs for later years.

Then comes a silence of eighteen years. Many novelists, authors, historians, poets and playwrights have tried to fill it in. They have imagined the Holy Family in Nazareth, Jesus attending the synagogue school, growing from puberty to adolescence and young manhood, helping his father in the carpenter shop. Somewhere in those silent years Joseph died: and Jesus became the village carpenter, the man of the family, responsible for his mother and brothers and sisters. Surely he was a good carpenter, a skilled craftsman, honest and reliable, a true source of security for his family. Then one day he shocked all of them by closing the door and leaving the carpenter shop forever. That must have hurt Mary, though her love followed him in his new career, and she understood him as no one else could.

The Suffering Mother

In the record of Jesus' ministry Mary first appears at a wedding reception in Cana-of-Galilee. Jesus and his disciples are among the guests. When a practical crisis arises, Mary turns instinctively to her practical son. "They have no wine left," she says. At some weddings that would be more than a crisis; it would be a disaster. Jesus returns what has always seemed to be a harsh answer, "O woman, what have you to do with me?" (R.S.V.) but which the New English Bible softens, "Your concern, mother, is not mine." Mary recognises her son's authority and says to the servants, "Do whatever he tells you."[9]

The worst day in Mary's life, next to Good Friday, must have been the Sabbath when Jesus preached in his home synagogue at Nazareth. It should have been a proud day for his family and for the whole town. By that time Jesus had made Nazareth famous. According to Luke's Gospel the congregation did react proudly at first. "There was a general stir of admiration; they were surprised that words of such grace should fall from his lips."[10] Mark finds the people in a different mood. They were indignant that this young upstart, who only a few months ago was mending their tables and chairs and making yokes for oxen, should be standing up and preaching to them like a rabbi. "Is not this the carpenter, the son of Mary..."[11] That put Mary in her place. In Luke's Gospel their mood changed very quickly. They were so offended by Jesus' sermon that they threw him out of town and took him to a steep cliff, known today as the Mount of Precipitation, intending to hurl him over the edge.[12] Jesus escaped but undoubtedly left his family with an acute sense of embarrassment and public disgrace. A sword really pierced his mother's heart that day.

Many of Jesus' sayings must have been hard on his mother. There was the day when she and his brothers sent a message that they wanted to see him, and he said to the crowd, "My mother and my brothers — they are those who hear the word of God and act upon it."[13] There was a day when a woman cried out, in effect, "You have made your mother a happy woman," and Jesus replied, "No, happy are those who hear the word of God and keep it."[14] There was the day when he said to a great crowd, "If anyone comes to me and does not hate his father and mother, wife and children, brothers and sisters, even his own life, he cannot be a disciple of mine."[15] All those sayings must have been like a sword that pierced the heart of the suffering mother.

At this point Mary disappears from Luke's Gospel, and from Matthew and Mark, though not from Luke's narrative, because he finds her with the disciples and with Jesus' brothers in the Upper Room after the Ascension.[16] John now takes up the Gospel story of Mary, and with good reason, because he becomes personally involved in it. The scene is "the highest hill," the Hill of Calvary where Jesus hangs crucified between two thieves, beaten, shamed, mocked and spat upon, his life blood slowly ebbing away. Near the cross stands Mary, his mother. She has always known that it would come to this, but she has loved him, and her love has followed him to the very end. She is not an old woman, perhaps forty-nine or fifty, but she looks old and tired and ready to die in the terrible moment of her son's agony. It is her body that hangs on that cross, battered and mangled. She hears the words of tender concern entrusting her to the care of John, the beloved disciple who, according to tradition, became a son to her and later took her with him to Ephesus. But nothing on Calvary can soften the pain of her sword-pierced heart. Poor little maiden mother! You will sing the Magnificat again on Easter Sunday but right now you are suffering as only a mother can suffer with her son.[17]

Beneath the Church of the Annunciation at Nazareth is a grotto, believed to be the site of Mary's encounter with the Angel Gabriel. I once conducted worship in that grotto and, as I read aloud the story from Luke's Gospel, I suddenly realized that to me the real miracle is not that Jesus was conceived without the aid of a human father but that God chose as the earthly mother of his Son a humble village maiden who accepted and fulfilled that exalted role with perfect obedience and love. Standing there in the grotto I bowed my head and offered a prayer that I can't remember now but that must have gone like this:

Dear God, thank you for choosing a humble village maiden to be the Mother of your Son. Thank you that she has shown us the way of perfect obedience to your will. Thank you for watching over her on that cold and perilous night in Bethlehem long ago. Thank you that Mary and Joseph were loving and supportive parents to your Son. May we also be loving and supportive parents to the children whom you have entrusted to our care. Make us ready to obey your will and let us feel secure in the knowledge that you have shared our life and are with us always; through the living presence of Jesus Christ, your Son, our Saviour. Amen.

CHAPTER NOTES.

1. Luke 1:26-35
2. Luke 1:38
3. Luke 1:46-53
4. Luke 2:1-20
5. Luke 2:22-38
6. Matt. 2:16-23
7. Luke 2:40
8. Luke 2:41-52
9. John 2:1-11
10. Luke 4:22
11. Mark 6:3
12. Luke 4:23-30
13. Luke 8:19-21
14. Luke 11:27-28
15. Luke 14:24-27
16. Acts 1:12-14
17. John 19:25-27

2
Joseph

IN MATTHEW'S ACCOUNT of the Christmas story Joseph, not Mary, is the central supporting character. Matthew was a Jewish writer who wrote his Gospel for Jews. He wanted above all else to establish that Jesus was a Jew and to prove that he was the Messiah of Jewish expectation. Jews traced a man's ancestry through his father. Therefore Matthew begins his genealogy of Jesus with Abraham, the father of the Hebrew race, and brings it down forty-two generations to Joseph. He does not say that Joseph was the biological father of Jesus but describes him as "the husband of Mary who gave birth to Jesus called Messiah."[1] What would Joseph say to that? Listen to his soliloquy:

There is more than one way of being a parent and of not being a parent. A man may co-operate in the creation of a child and never be a true father to that child at all. It happens all the time. Another man may be the best kind of father to a little one whom God has entrusted to his care. If it is a father's role to take a child and accept responsibility for him, to guard him against danger, to give him a home and surround him with love, to feed and clothe him, to be his companion and to teach and train him so that he grows up to be a complete person — if that is a father's role, then Jesus was my son too, and I shall not believe otherwise.

You know that my name is Joseph but you don't know very much about me. I played only a small supporting role in the larger Gospel drama. The centuries have quite properly allowed me to be eclipsed by my wondrous son and overshadowed by my beautiful and innocent wife. But I played a major role in the event which you celebrate at Christmas. I remember Bethlehem vividly and, though I did not understand it fully at the time, I would like to tell you about it now.

I myself was born in Bethlehem. My father, Jacob, was a carpenter, the son of a long line of carpenters. At the time of my birth he had a small shop in the village where he built furniture for the wealthy citizens of Jerusalem. But father was a humble man who liked and understood humble people. He used to tell my mother that he would be much happier working in a smaller community where the people had simpler needs. Hearing that the 'town carpenter in Nazareth of Galilee had died, he decided to move north and go into business there. I was five years old at the time.

Father built up a flourishing trade in Nazareth as the years passed, and when I came of age he took me into the shop as an apprentice. After his death I became the village carpenter and began thinking of marriage so that sons might be born to carry on our heritage. One day, having gone to Sepphoris in search of lumber, I stopped to call upon a friend and by the Providence of God was introduced to Mary.

Mary! Sweet, gracious, lovely, innocent Mary! God never made a more beautiful and perfect creature, not even before the Garden of Eden. Forgive me if I become emotional at the very mention of her name. I loved her at first sight. My heart fairly throbbed to make her my wife. Yet even then I knew that something deeper than love bound us together, some deed which we could do for God and which no one else could do, a purpose that she and I were meant to share together. My joy knew no bounds when one day Mary lifted her sweet face and said simply to my clumsy, faltering proposal, "Yes, Joseph, I love you and I will be your wife." So we were betrothed and our wedding arranged for a suitable date.

Then, without warning, my happiness was shattered into a thousand pieces. Have you ever tried to imagine yourself dying, so that you could almost feel the cold, frigid darkness, your breath stopping in your throat, your brain numbed by shock? That's how I felt when Mary, whom I would have trusted to the ends of the earth, confessed that she was expecting a child, not my child. "This isn't true!" I kept saying to myself. "This is a ghastly nightmare. I shall waken in a moment, and all will be well again." What was I to do? Mary had been unfaithful to me. If I chose to make a public spectacle of her, she could be stoned to death; that was the penalty for adultery. As "a man of principle" — so the Bible describes me — I had no moral choice but to break the engagement. Yet I wanted to save Mary from exposure because I still loved her and would never stop loving her. We made plans for her to go to Hebron and stay with her relative, Elizabeth, and have the baby there. Then I had the marriage contract quietly set aside and told our families and friends that we had changed our minds about each other.[2] It seemed the right thing to do at the time.

The right thing and the end of the world! Oh, the agony, the tortured days and sleepless nights! My life was finished. I could never love anyone else but Mary. Nazareth was empty and my heart was empty without her. "Why, O God, did you let this happen?" I prayed over and over again. I must have fallen asleep on my knees one night, for I dreamed that God answered me. I dreamed that an angel stood beside me and said, "Joseph...do not be afraid to take Mary home with you as your wife. It is by the Holy Spirit that she has conceived this child. She will bear a son, and you shall give him the name Jesus (Saviour), for he will save his people from their sins."[3] I lay awake in the morning for a long time thinking. Could this be the Divine purpose that Mary and I were meant to share? I closed the carpenter shop, followed her to Hebron, took her in my arms and asked her forgiveness. "Oh Joseph," she cried when I told her, "now you understand. Now I can tell you the secret which has been locked up in my heart. I, too, had a heavenly vision. This *is* God's Son. 'He will be great,' the angel said; 'the Lord God will give him the throne of his ancestor David, and he will be king over Israel for ever; his reign shall never end.' "[4]

So Mary and I were married. I brought her home to Nazareth, to the little house behind the carpenter's shop.[5] Our happiness was nearly complete. No man could have wished for a more loving and devoted wife. She was so patient and gentle, she kept the house so tidy and comfortable, she received our friends so graciously. They all loved her and expressed their joy that we were soon to be blessed with the arrival of a child. But I must confess that I had mixed feelings in those days. Toward Mary I felt only tenderness, but there were times when the vision of the angel seemed far away, and I wondered if, when the time came, I could measure up to all that God expected of me.

Then came the ridiculous order from the Emperor Caesar Augustus. Each Jewish citizen must go to the town of his birth to be registered.[6] For me that meant Bethlehem, a hundred-mile journey, six days by donkey over barren, mountainous land. Mary didn't have to come, and I begged her to stay at home with her time so near, but she insisted that we be together. It was a gruelling journey for her. She must have suffered terribly; though every time I looked at her I saw a smile on her face and the light of happy expectation in her eyes. She did her best to calm my fears about the baby. "He will come when God intends that he should come," she said confidently; and added, "If he should come while we are still in Bethlehem, then all the more reason for believing that he will one day be a king as David was before him. Yes," she mused, "it would be good to have a King born in King David's city."

By mid-afternoon of the sixth day I knew that Mary might have her wish fulfilled. My one prayer was that we should reach the town before her pains became too frequent and unbearable. "Thanks be to God," I cried out, as we entered Bethlehem at nightfall. "See, Mary, there is an inn not far from here. I remember it well. My father built some furniture for it when I was a boy. Perhaps the innkeeper will remember my name. You will be comfortable and well cared for there." I had forgotten that Bethlehem would be full of travellers that night. All day long they had been arriving for the enrollment, and the innkeeper had long since posted his "No Vacancy" sign; even his own family quarters had been turned over to guests. "I'm truly sorry," he said when he saw how desperate was our predicament, "but you won't find an empty room anywhere in Bethlehem tonight. And it's such a cold night! If only you had come earlier!" What were we to do? "Merciful God," I prayed in panic. "If this child is your Son, don't let him die like a dog at the side of the road. Have pity on him for his mother's sake."

I believe it was God who led us to the stable. We found it on the edge of town, a rough wooden structure built in a sort of cave in the side of a hill. I exclaimed bitterly, "Even the animals have a roof over their heads, a place to lie down in the straw!" Through her pain Mary whispered, "Perhaps the animals will not turn us away." Nor did they turn us away. They stood there silently as I entered the cave and began to spread coverings across the hay. I made a bed for Mary and then hurried out to get food and water and to bring back, if I could find her, a woman who might help Mary in her time of need. It must have taken longer than I expected, because when I entered the cave again, our baby had been born. Warmly nestled in his mother's arms, our little Jesus had come safely into the world of men.

Oh the inexpressible tenderness that flooded my soul in that sacred moment! Is there anything in all the world more appealing in its utter helplessness than a new-born infant? A single blunder, and we might have snuffed out that little wisp of life there and then. God's Son or my son, he was a baby born of a woman, as tiny and helpless as any other new-born child. Someone would have to be his earthly father, someone surround him with the strong arms of love and protection; and if I didn't do it, who would? As he began to whimper, I fell to my knees in thanksgiving to God. "Truly God, thou art the Creator of all life," I prayed, "and thou hast entrusted to my keeping this precious baby and his mother. Help me to be worthy of this trust and give me the wisdom and the strength to fulfil it."

We had unexpected visitors that night, some shepherds from the nearby hills. As I stepped outside to meet them I noticed how bright and clear the stars shone. Right above the stable one star shone more brightly than all the rest. The shepherds said that they had come to see the baby and they told a fantastic story of an angel who suddenly stood before them while they were taking care of the sheep. The sight terrified them, but the angel spoke, "Do not be afraid; I have good news for you: there is great joy coming to the whole

people. Today in the city of David a deliverer has been born
to you — the Messiah, the Lord." The angel went on to say,
"And this is your sign: you will find a baby lying wrapped in
his swaddling clothes, in a manger." The shepherds told me
that all at once the angel was surrounded by a great choir of
angels singing the praises of God and proclaiming peace
among men. So they came to Bethlehem as fast as they could.
They stepped inside the stable. They walked softly over to the
manger, looked closely at the baby, smiled at one another,
then knelt down on the dirt floor. They knelt before our little
Jesus as though they were worshipping him, almost as though
he were God. [7]

Was he God, the Son of God, the Messiah, the Saviour of
the world? It didn't seem possible according to everything I
had ever believed. If this little, squirming bit of pink flesh,
nestled at his mother's breast, were Almighty God, then it
was a new kind of Almightiness, and I would have to change
a lot of my ideas. What strange plan for mankind did God
hope to set in motion by coming to earth as a helpless baby in
these crude surroundings in this far-away corner of the world?
I tried to think about it, but it was all too much for my
uneducated mind.

We stayed for a while in Bethlehem. Most of the travellers
had left, and the innkeeper invited us to lodge in his house.
He and his wife made a great fuss over the baby. They could
not have been more kind. One day we had visitors not at all
like the humble shepherds. They rode camels and wore rich
clothing and told us that they were astrologers from eastern
countries who had come in search of a child born to be king
of the Jews. A great new star in the sky led them to
Bethlehem. When they saw our little Jesus they bowed to the
ground before him and presented him with gold, frankincense
and myrrh, gifts fit for a king. Was he a King, even then?
Mary accepted the gifts graciously. I didn't know what to say.
I was worried when the wise men, as they were leaving,
warned me to protect my child against the wrath of King
Herod in Jerusalem. [8]

That night God spoke to me in a dream. Like my ancestor,
also named Joseph, I was a man who dreamed; and it was
through my dreams that God continually directed me to fulfil

a protecting role, a fatherly role toward our child and his mother. He warned me of Herod's murderous intention toward Jesus and ordered us to leave for Egypt without a moment's delay. For more than a year we lived as refugees in that foreign land. With some difficulty I manged to find work so that I could earn money for the support of my little family. Twice more God spoke to me through dreams, and at last I knew that it was safe for us to go back to our home in Nazareth.[9]

You don't hear much about me after that. I disappear from the Gospel story. I did not live to see Jesus grown to manhood. I missed the great drama of his ministry on earth. Yet surely I helped to prepare him for that ministry. Thank God that I lived long enough to be a father to him in the years that really mattered, the formative years of his childhood and youth. I think I must have been a good father, or he would not have used the word "father" to describe God. We worked together in the carpenter shop. He used to help me when he was a lad and later became an apprentice, learning the trade from me as I had learned it from my father. We were very close in those days. We became good friends. I taught Jesus what I thought was going to be his life's work, but maybe the lessons I taught him about life itself were more important.

You ask me what he was like growing up as a child. In many ways he was like other children, yet unlike them because he thought and spoke with a wisdom far beyond his years. The Gospel says that he lived under my authority, but I often wondered which of us had the real authority, which was the father and which was the son. He was a mature child, especially in his relationship to other people; he was kind and generous and considerate. He was also deeply spiritual, he lived very close to God. How well I remember his twelfth birthday when we lost him in Jerusalem, then found him in the temple where he spoke of being in his Father's house.[10] Yes, God was his Father, and he was God's Son, for God lived in him as he has never lived so completely in another person on this earth.

But he was my son too. Just as surely as your boys and girls are yours today, Jesus was mine in Bethlehem, in Egypt and in the home and the carpenter's shop at Nazareth. And if I take a father's pride in him, let only fathers say that I am wrong. But don't misinterpret my pride. It springs not from any accomplishment of mine but only from the fact that God could choose a village maiden like Mary to be the mother of his greatest gift to men, that he could entrust a village carpenter like me with the care of his Incarnate Son, that he could pick a Bethlehem stable as the place in which the King of Kings should be born. I think God must love the children of earth very much that he should have been willing to draw so close to them.

CHAPTER NOTES:

1. Matt. 1:1-17
2. Matt. 1:18-19
3. Matt. 1:20-21
4. Luke 1:32-33
5. Matt. 1:24-25
6. Luke 2:1-7
7. Luke 2:8-20
8. Matt. 2:1-12
9. Matt. 2:13-23
10. Luke 2:44-52

3
Herod the Great

The Villain of the Christmas Drama

THERE HAS TO be at least one villain in every drama to round out the plot and create the element of conflict. The villain in the Christmas drama is the Jewish king, Herod the Great. He can scarcely be called a supporting character of Jesus. A man who tries to murder you doesn't support you. He prepared the way for Jesus only by getting out of the way. In fact, we wonder why history has named him Herod the Great. Great men don't go around killing little babies.

The Herod whom we know from his one appearance in the Bible story[1] may not have been great, but there was a time, especially in his early life, when he seemed to have the qualities that make for greatness. In his prime he was one of the world's most successful and notable men, a personal friend of Antony and Augustus Caesar. He once entertained Cleopatra in his palace — or maybe she entertained him. As a young man he had everything going for him. He was physically handsome, skilled in war, courageous in battle, shrewd in the arts of diplomacy, a born leader of men. As a reward for his services to Rome the Roman Senate made him King of Judea before he was thirty years of age, an office which he held for more than forty years.

Herod was not only a strong king at first but a comparatively good king. Though not a Jew, he got along well with the Jews and knew how to manage them. To consolidate his position he married a Jewish heiresss, Mariamne, whom he loved with passionate devotion. Unfortunately her family treated him with contempt as a low-born foreigner, and he hated them for it. Nevertheless, he won the admiration and almost the love of his subjects. He could be generous. In a time of famine he stripped his palace of gold and silver to buy corn. In prosperous times he initiated some impressive building projects — an amphitheatre and hippodrome, parks and palaces in Jerusalem. He built the harbour of Caesarea, named in honour of the Emperor, and the city of Sebaste in honour of the Emperor's wife. Their excavated ruins today testify to their magnificence. Though not a religious man, Herod respected the Jewish religion. His greatest work was the reconstruction of the Jewish temple in Jerusalem on a grander scale than that built by Solomon. In many ways he could have been a second Solomon.

Analysing Herod's weakness, some historians call him unscrupulous and ambitious. Basically he was an insecure man. That was why he put down all opposition with ruthless severity. He dealt with political opponents as any absolute monarch in those days dealt with them. He also dealt harshly with what he thought was disloyalty in his own family. To please Mariamne he appointed her brother high priest, but when that person became too popular, he had him put to death. Mariamne never forgave him, and later in a fit of rage he ordered her execution — for which he never forgave himself and for which he suffered in body and mind.

That seems to be the turning-point in Herod's career. After the murder of his wife his character disintegrated completely. Like Shakespeare's Macbeth he had killed for the sake of expediency, but now he killed for the sake of killing. He became a butcher. Formerly he distrusted his enemies, but now he distrusted even the people closest to him. With no compunction he ordered the execution of his two sons by Mariamne. He wanted no rival to his throne. Augustus said that it was better to be Herod's pig than his son.

The Butcher of Bethlehem

That was the man who governed Judea when Jesus was born; an old man, past seventy years of age, with haunting and embittered memories, the blood of his own wife and sons upon his hands; an old man, proud, watchful and implacable.

You can just imagine his dark and crafty thoughts when astrologers from the east came one day to Jerusalem, asking people, "Where is the child who is to be born king of the Jews? We observed the rising of his star, and we have come to pay him homage." No wonder Herod was perturbed. He thought he had eliminated all possible pretenders to his throne. No wonder the whole of Jerusalem was perturbed with him. It would be correct to say that all Jerusalem trembled. His courtiers must have wondered if he would allow the astrologers to leave the city alive. But Herod was smarter than that. He called a conference of the chief priests and lawyers of the Jews and asked them to tell him where it was prophesied that the Messiah should be born. They replied, "In Bethlehem." Next day Herod summoned the astrologers to a private audience and, when he learned that they had been guided by a star, he sent them to Bethlehem, saying, "Go and make a careful inquiry for the child. When you have found him, report to me, so that I may go myself and pay him homage."

Herod should have known that the astrologers were just as smart as he was. They were not called "wise men" for nothing. They knew the Jewish king by reputation. They knew how he disposed of his rivals. They knew also, when they saw the baby nestled in his mother's arms, that if the child grew to manhood he would be Herod's greatest rival. They knew *that* when they presented their costly gifts of gold, frankincense and myrrh, gifts fit for a King, but gifts that they would never have presented to Herod. They knew that Herod, being what he was, and the child, being what he was, the two were destined to come into conflict.

The conflict came sooner than expected. When the astrologers did not return to Jerusalem, and when Herod learned that they had tricked him and taken another route to their own countries he went berserk. By this time he had convinced himself that the baby born in Bethlehem was, in fact, the Messiah who would one day be King of the Jews. There couldn't be two kings of the Jews. Therefore one had to be eliminated. Herod devised a maniacal scheme to accomplish that dark purpose. In a fit of rage he sent a squad of armed soldiers with orders to massacre all male children two years of age and under, in the region of Bethlehem. It is estimated that some twenty infants were killed in the massacre. We have no other historical account of the event apart from Matthew's Gospel but we don't doubt its truth. It was the sort of thing that Herod would have done. He was behaving true to form and entirely consistently with his character especially during the later years of his life. He was the villain in the Christmas drama.

The Only Realist

A villain to be sure, but also the only realist in the Christmas Drama. Call him a liar, an infanticidal maniac, he nevertheless recognised that the event which took place on Christmas Day constituted a threat to himself and all that he stood for. Great Caesar on his throne, the high priest in Jerusalem, the brigands in the hills, the merchants in the market place — none of them would have recognised the Babe of Bethlehem as a threat to their interests. If any of them had stepped into the stable on the night when Jesus was born they would doubtless have smiled good-naturedly at the babe lying in Mary's arms. They had nothing to fear from a baby. Of course, neither did Herod think that he had anything to fear from a baby. He alone recognised the obvious fact that the baby might grow up and become a man.

He did grow up and become a man, a strong, magnetic, controversial man. The Babe of Bethlehem became the Man of Nazareth; and when that happened, his contemporaries did not smile at him quite so good-naturedly. To such men as Caiaphas and Pilate, leading men of affairs, authoritative men in church and state, the man Jesus seemed intolerable. He offended their prejudices, he challenged their conventions, he set up standards of right and wrong which blasted their respectability. He held forth principles of life which every stubborn instinct in them rejected. Those who knew the Man Jesus some thirty years after his birth in Bethlehem believed sincerely that there was nothing which their world needed so much as to have him die. Herod just happened to be a jump ahead of them. He had no fear of a baby lying in a cave among sheep and oxen; it was simply that he had sufficient foresight to visualise the man that this baby would eventually become. Best to murder him at the start! Get him out of the way! Liquidate him! Under no circumstances must the child be allowed to grow up.

The child grew up, and Herod died. The crazy king failed in his maniacal scheme to murder God's Messiah. Even as the soldiers with naked swords were on their way to Bethlehem, God spoke to Joseph in a dream and instructed him to take the child and his mother and leave immediately for Egypt. Who warned the parents of the other children? Did they have dreams too? Or did they have only nightmares for the rest of their lives as they lived with the memory of those flashing blades that cut down their infants and toddlers like sheaves of grain? Surely those were the first Christian martyrs, the first who died for Jesus. Surely God gave them a special place in heaven! Meanwhile the Holy Family remained in Egypt until Joseph had another dream in which God said, "Rise up, take the child and his mother, and go with them to the land of Israel, for the men who threatened the child's life are dead."

Herod died a lonely and horrible death through cancer. The story has it that, as his death drew near, he began to worry that there would be no one to mourn him, so he devised another of his fiendish schemes. He had a number of Jews locked in the Hippodrome and gave orders that, the moment he died, they were to be slaughtered, so that all Jerusalem would hear their screaming and wailing and think that it was for him. At the last he suffered such violent pain that he tried to end it all by committing suicide. Just then he learned that his eldest son, anticipating his father's death, had seized the throne; and Herod ordered his execution as the last atrocity of a dying man. When the cruel king finally stopped breathing, the whole realm began to breathe again as though the shadow of a long fear had been lifted.

A Philosophy of History

"The men who threatened the child's life are dead." There is a philosophy of history in those words. You can sum it up by saying that God finishes the Christmas story. The Herods die, and Jesus lives. Of course, it's a biological fact that old men die and babies grow up, if their parents can keep them warm and properly fed. It is also a recurring judgment of history. In every century there have been Herods who, recognising the Incarnate Son of God as a threat to all that they stood for, have tried to murder him in his cradle. One of them by the same name tried to persecute the infant Church out of existence. He murdered James, the brother of John. He imprisoned Peter, intending to execute him also. He became drunk with illusions of his own divinity. He was eaten up with worms and died.[2] Herod died, and Jesus lived. God finished the story.

In the first three centuries a succession of "Herods" sat on the throne of the world in Rome. They all devised maniacal schemes to kill the Church in its infancy. For Christians it was a time of bitter and bloody persecution. They were socially ostracised, politically disenfranchised, ecclesiastically scorned and economically impoverished. They were dubbed atheists, derided as haters of the human race and falsely charged with perpetrating the grossest immoralities. One Roman Emperor ordered some of them to be wrapped in the hides of wild beasts and torn to pieces by dogs. Others he fastened to crosses and set on fire to illuminate a circus staged for the crowds in his own gardens. The ruins of that great world building, the Coliseum, stand today in Rome as the enduring symbol of the torture and death suffered at the hands of Herod by any man or woman who dared to acknowledge the sovereignty of Christ. Yet Herod died, and Christ lived. Again God finished the story. As early as the year A.D. 403 you could read this telling paragraph in a letter of Jerome:

> Even in Rome itself paganism is left in solitude. The Egyptian Serapis has become a Christian. The Huns have learned the Psalter. The chilly Cynthians are warmed by the faith. Every pagan temple in Rome is covered with cobwebs. They who once were the gods of the nation remain under their leaking, lonely roofs with horned owls and other birds of the night.

German Naziism was a reincarnation of Herod. Hitler passed no laws against the celebration of Christmas. He saw no threat in the worship of the Holy Child Jesus, no conflict between National Socialism and infantile Christianity. He was less benevolent toward the mature religion of the Man of Galilee. He wanted in the land no Churches that still proclaimed the sovereignty of God, the dignity of the individual, the brotherhood of all men and the rule of love over hate. People who proclaimed that uncompromising Gospel were thrown into concentration camps. Yet some of them persisted in their beliefs and wrote them down on any paper they could find, even toilet paper. It could truthfully be said that we had this treasure in earthen vessels. One of them was Dietrich Bonhoeffer. The letters, papers and manuscripts that he wrote before his execution were somehow smuggled out of prison and have since been recognised as some of the most influential theological documents of our time. Again Herod died. Again Jesus lives. Again God finished the story.

There will always be Herods on a grand scale or a petty scale, some like the tiger, others like the jackal. In politics, business, culture and all areas of life there are people who recognise their incompatibility with Jesus. They know, better than we know, that he represents principles so utterly different from their own, that the two kingdoms cannot possibly exist at the same time and in the same place. There is not room in the world for both. Therefore one must go, and they are determined that Jesus shall go. They may not employ the crude and violent methods of the King of Judea. Never be so vulgar and lawless as to cut off the baby's head. Smother him instead, starve him to death, create a climate of cynicism, ridicule, hedonism and materialism in which a spiritual interpretation of life cannot possibly survive. We sometimes feel overpowered by the Herods of our society, the dictators, the diplomats, the politicians, the journalists, the broadcasters, the manipulators of men's bodies and minds who seem totally dedicated to the destruction of all that the Church stands for. Against them we have no defence. We can only wait for them to die, wait for God to finish the story.

From Death to Life

Must the story always end with the death of Herod? No, not always. There was another Herod who tried to kill God's

Messiah. His name was Saul of Tarsus. The New Testament
says that after giving his approval to the stoning of Stephen,
he was "harrying the church; he entered house after house,
seizing men and women, and sending them to prison."[3] Saul
of Tarsus was Christianity's public enemy number one.
Unless he were eliminated from the scene, the young Church
was doomed to die in its infancy. We can forgive the early
Christians if, remembering the huge jagged rocks that
pounded the dying Stephen to a pulp, they had prayed
fiercely, "God, let a brick fall on the head of Saul of Tarsus."
God answered their prayer more marvellously than they
could ever have dreamed. He did not eliminate Saul, he
converted him. He hit him not with a brick but with the
power of the living Christ.[4] God killed Saul the Pharisee and
brought to life Paul the Apostle, the greatest single figure
responsible for Christianity's growth to a mature and independent world religion. That's how God finished *that* story. It
is a story that ended not in death but in life.

So it might have ended for Herod the Great. Suppose
Herod had meant it when he said to the astrologers, "Go, and
make a careful inquiry for the child. When you have found
him, report to me, so that I may go myself and pay him
homage"? Suppose Herod had gone to Bethlehem and
entered the house and knelt down and placed his crown
beside the gold, frankincense and myrrh at the feet of the
Holy Child Jesus? He might not have cancelled a life of crime
but he might have found what he had been looking for all his
life — forgiveness, peace and salvation. He might still have
died of cancer but died to live again.

CHAPTER NOTES:

1. Matt. 2:1-23   3. Acts 8:3
2. Acts 12:18-23   4. Acts 9:1-22

4
John the Baptist

A Play within the Play

WE NOMINATED MARY, the mother of Jesus, as the best
supporting character in the Christian drama. Jesus himself
nominated John the Baptist, an unusual character who might
be called a first-century hippie, the patron saint of all hippies.
He looked the part with his long hair and uncombed beard.
He wore a rough coat of camel's hair with a leather belt
around his waist and open sandals on his feet. He dropped
out of normal society, joined a commune and lived a life of
voluntary poverty. He protested against the values of a
bourgeois culture. But there the similarity stops, because
John was not concerned with doing his own thing. He was
concerned with doing God's thing and with leading other
people to it. That's what earned for him the finest tribute
that Jesus ever paid to any man: *"Never has there appeared on
earth a mother's son greater than John the Baptist, and yet the least in
the kingdom of Heaven is greater than he."* [1]

Around John himself we can weave a fascinating drama in
four acts, a play within the play. Act One has three scenes.
The first is a set in the temple at Jerusalem. The Angel
Gabriel appears to an elderly priest named Zechariah and
tells him that his wife Elizabeth is going to have a baby who
will grow up to be a great prophet whose vocation will be "to
prepare a people that shall be fit for the Lord." [2] Zechariah
doesn't doubt the big thing but he does doubt the little thing.
He tells the angel that he and his wife are too old to have a
baby. Gabriel tells him that the tongue which expressed such
doubts will be silenced until the day of the baby's birth.

The second scene takes place at Zechariah's home in the Judean hills. The impossible has happened — the aged Elizabeth is pregnant. One day she is visited by a young woman from Galilee named Mary who also is expecting a child. As the two women meet, the foetus suddenly stirs in Elizabeth's womb, as if in adoration, and she says humbly, "Who am I, that the mother of my Lord should visit me?"[3]

The third scene takes us back to the temple. Elizabeth's baby has been born, and they have brought him to be circumcised. His relatives think he should be named Zechariah Junior, but the old priest writes on a tablet, "His name is John"; and with that he begins speaking again, to the astonishment of all the people who ask, "What will this child become?"[4] Zechariah knows what he shall become. He sings of it in praise to God: "And you, my child, you shall be called the Prophet of the Highest, for you will be the Lord's forerunner to prepare his way."[5]

The scene in Act Two is set in the Judean wilderness on the bank of the River Jordan. A huge congregation listens intently to the preaching of a prophet, the first authentic prophet to appear in Israel for three centuries. He preaches all over Judea and draws crowds wherever he goes. This is John grown to manhood. For the best part of thirty years he has been living in a monastic community near the Dead Sea. Now he presents an awesome appearance with his lean, ascetic features and his flashing eyes. Even the robbers are afraid of him. He preaches fearlessly to the people, especially to the religious leaders. He calls them vipers, warns them against the coming judgment of God, summons them to repent and be baptised as a sign of their repentance. "Already the axe is laid to the roots of the trees; and every tree that fails to produce good fruit is cut down and thrown into the fire." John demands that they prove their repentance; and when they ask, "What are we to do?" he tells them to begin by practising the common virtues of kindness, honesty and courtesy. The people wonder if he can be the promised Messiah, but he says, "No...there is one to come who is mightier than I... He will baptise you with the Holy Spirit and with fire."[6] Even as John preaches and baptises, the Messiah does come. John recognises him standing in the water beside him and exclaims, "I need rather to be baptised by you." Jesus insists on being baptised by John. As he emerges from the water, a voice from heaven is heard saying, "This is my Son, my Beloved, on whom my favour rests."[7]

Act Three has four scenes. In scene one a deputation of religious leaders comes to John at Bethany and asks if he is the Messiah. When he says, "No", they ask why he is baptising. He replies, "I baptise in water, but among you, though you do not know him, stands the one who is to come after me. I am not good enough to unfasten his shoes."[8]

In scenes two and three John sees Jesus coming toward him. He recalls the visitation of the Holy Spirit in his baptism and points to him as "God's chosen one...the Lamb of God...who takes away the sin of the world." Next day John points two of his followers to Jesus and again says, "There is the Lamb of God." The two men leave their master and follow Jesus.[9]

Scene four takes place near the Jordan River several weeks or months later. John's disciples come to him with the disturbing news that he now has a rival. They tell him that Jesus also is baptising and drawing bigger crowds. That doesn't disturb John. He has been expecting it, he sees it as God's plan, and it fills his heart with joy. It is the joy of the best man at a wedding, the joy of fading into the background and giving glory to the bridegroom. Jesus is the bridegroom. With fine humility John says concerning him, "As he grows greater, I must grow less."[10]

John himself does not appear in the first scene of Act Four. It takes place up in Galilee mid-way through Jesus' ministry. One day he receives messengers from John who bring a strange question: "Are you the one who is to come, or are we to expect some other?" Is this John speaking — he who heard the voice at the baptism and heralded Jesus as the promised Messiah? What can have happened to create such doubt in his mind? We can only guess that his own morale has been brought low, because he has been in prison for a while, put there by the foxy King Herod Antipas whose adulterous marriage he condemned. Also he has heard that Jesus is not proceeding according to plan. Instead of swinging an axe at sinners, he is forgiving them and healing the sick. How can he be the Messiah? Jesus instructs the messengers to tell John that works of mercy are exactly what make him the Messiah.

Then he turns to the crowds and speaks highly of John and pays him the supreme tribute, "Never has there appeared on earth a mother's son greater than John the Baptist, and yet the least in the kingdom of Heaven is greater than he."[11]

The final scene, set in the palace of King Herod near Jerusalem, is one of the most colourful and exciting in all Scripture. It has everything that delights the hearts of motion picture producers — music, dancing, feasting, drunkenness, intrigue, violence, murder and sex. The occasion is Herod's birthday party during which his step-daughter, Salome, does a strip-tease that so inflames the old lecher that he swears an oath to give her anything she asks — up to half his kingdom. Prompted by her scheming mother, Herod's wife, she asks for the head of John the Baptist. That sobers up the king and distresses him. He respects John and has often conversed with him privately and has kept him in prison mainly to protect him against his vengeful wife. However, he has sworn an oath and he has to stick by it. Screams fill the air when the executioner re-enters the banquet hall carrying a man's head on a meat platter. John's disciples later come for his body and carry it away sorrowfully for burial.[12]

The Greatest

Outside modern Jerusalem is the little village of Ein Karem, remembered as the birthplace of John the Baptist. On the entrance of a beautiful church is a German inscription which recalls the role played by this best supporting character in the Christian drama. It reads,

> Let me prepare the way for thee,
> Remove each stone that might hinder thee
> To make thy coming sure and soon.

That was the man of whom Jesus said, "Never has there appeared on earth a mother's son greater than John the Baptist." In what did his greatness lie? He was a great prophet, the last of the great prophets. He stood in the prophetic tradition of Elijah, Amos, Isaiah and Jeremiah, all of whom pointed to the coming of Christ. Only John touched Christ, literally touched him, and was therefore a bridge-character between the Old and New Testaments. Moreover,

John recognised Jesus for what he was. It needed no miracles, no matchless teaching, no mighty works, no Cross and no Resurrection to convince him that Jesus was the promised Messiah of Israel. Others came gradually to that recognition. They saw God in Jesus only when they had exhausted all human categories. John saw God in Jesus from the very beginning. Don't contrast him unfavourably with the other disciples. He begins where they end. He is ahead of them all.

John's true greatness lay in his self-effacement. He was not only a prophet but a phenomenally successful prophet. Never had any preacher achieved such acclaim. John had the world at his feet and could have posed as anyone, even the Messiah. He could have remained in the spotlight and claimed the glory for himself. But no! John didn't want the glory. He didn't want to usurp the place of the star in the drama. He wanted to be a supporting character. Time and again he told people, "I am only the forerunner. Your true Messiah is coming. Look to him." One day Jesus appeared on the scene, attracting the crowds away from John to himself, among them John's closest friends and disciples. John knew that his high hour was gone. The career, for which he had given up everything in life, was effectively finished. Yet John did not resent being eclipsed by Jesus. Instead, he pointed to Jesus and said with true self-effacement, "As he grows greater, I must grow less." If John the Baptist had never spoken another word in Scripture, that one would have marked him down as a saint.

The greatest role that any Christian can play is that of a supporting character to Jesus. A preacher tries to play that role, though he may not always succeed. He knows that preaching is not supposed to be an ego-trip and that if people come away from church saying, "Isn't he a great preacher and doesn't he preach great sermons?" he has failed miserably. A preacher has only one legitimate reason for being in the pulpit, only one purpose to which everything else must be subordinated. He must stand aside and let people see Jesus Christ. He must say concerning Jesus, "As he grows greater, I must grow less."

That is the purpose of every Christian's life, the essence of Christian witness. The self with all its egotism and pride must fade into the background, while Christ, the life of Christ within us, comes forward so that people can see him and be

attracted to him and serve him. That is the role of the
Church, a role easily forgotten in the Church's struggle for
statistical success. Some misguided magazines occasionally do
a rating on churches, trying to decide which ones are great
according to their own fallible criteria of membership,
budgets, outreach programmes, etc. They forget that there is
only one criterion of greatness for any church, large or small,
successful or unsuccessful: Does it prepare men and women to
meet Jesus Christ? That was the greatness of John the
Baptist.

Less than the Least

Yet Jesus qualified his tribute to John. Having said that
"never has there appeared on earth a mother's son greater
than John the Baptist", he added, "and yet the least in the
kingdom of Heaven is greater than he." That seems an almost
damning statement, as though to say that, good as he may be,
John isn't quite good enough. It seems a snobbish statement,
as though to say that the poorest Christian is better than the
best nonchristian — which the facts of life do not support at
all. John was not a Christian, in the sense that he didn't live
far into the Christian era, he never became one of the
disciples of Jesus, he never joined the Church. King Herod
didn't allow him the opportunity. Does that make him
inferior to Bartholomew or Thaddaeus or Peter or any of the
disciples? There had to be a more fundamental reason for
Jesus saying that John fell short of the kingdom of Heaven.

Go back to his ministry and listen again to his message:
"Already the axe is laid to the roots of the trees; and every tree
that fails to produce good fruit is cut down and thrown on the
fire... There is one to come who is mightier than I... His
shovel is ready in his hand to winnow the threshing-floor and
gather the wheat into his granary; but he will burn the chaff
on a fire that can never go out." That sounds like hell, doesn't
it? It sounds like the last judgment at the end of the age, the
human race separated into sheep and goats, good and bad; no
tolerance, no compromise, no middle ground; no place for the
wavering, no provision for the stunted, no tenderness for the
tempted. Judgment now! Do you wonder that John, having

proclaimed that stern, uncompromising message, should express doubt when Jesus began inviting to the Kingdom the very weaklings whom he had excluded? Do you wonder that Jesus, having inaugurated a Kingdom of love and mercy among men, could not include in it the narrowness and intolerance of John? That's why he said, "the least in the kingdom of Heaven is greater than he."

Yet Jesus wanted to include John in the kingdom. That's why he sent him so loving and patient a reply which we might paraphrase in our own words: "John you have lost your first faith in me. Because I don't fit into your pattern, you now doubt that I am the Messiah. You want to know if I am really the one who is to come, or should you look for another. My dear friend and cousin, it's because I don't fit into your pattern that I *am* the one who is to come. I am God's Messiah, not yours. You want me to chop down the fruitless trees and clear out the chaff from the threshing-floor and burn it on eternal fire. You want me to say, 'I see no blind here, no lame, no leper, no deaf, no poor and ignorant needing to be preached to.' But that's what I wish to see on the threshing-floor. I wish to see the very people whom you have put out — the blind, the lame, the leper, the deaf, the spiritually dead. And I don't want to put them out. I don't want to judge them now. I want to cleanse them and heal them."

One of the impressive modern statues of Christ is that by Thorvalsden which stands today behind the altar of the Protestant Cathedral in Copenhagen, Denmark. He worked on it for weeks and at last surveyed the finished product with satisfaction — a Christ with strong arms outstretched, raised high in gesturing command, and the fine-shaped head thrown back in triumph. "This is he," the artist said, "a powerful, majestic Christ." Thorvalsden closed the door of his studio for several days so that the day might set. When he returned and opened the door he stared in horror and disbelief. There had been a storm. Dampness had invaded the studio and altered the statue. No longer were the arms outstretched; now they fell low. The moisture had caused the once-proud head to bend. Gone was the triumph of Thorvalsden's Christ; he looked defeated now. For a long time the artist had no heart for work but finally he went with a friend to his studio again to see if somehow he might repair the damage and recapture the likeness of the strong Man of Galilee. They stopped and gazed in awe at the statue. Bathed in light, the lowered arms no longer depicted defeat; instead, they reached out with the compassion of God to sinful, sorrowing, suffering humanity. The head no longer seemed to droop; rather it bowed low with contrite countenance as if to say, "Come unto me, all ye that labour and are heavy laden, and I will give you rest." [13]

That had to happen to John's image of Jesus before he could enter Jesus' kingdom. Perhaps it did happen in Herod's damp dungeon where John was no longer part of the wheat but part of the chaff that he wanted Jesus to destroy. He had been like a man who never had an illness and who therefore could not sympathize with ill health. Now there sprang up in his soul a fellow-feeling with all illness, weakness and infirmity. Now he was identified with the human race, no longer a prophet but a person. Now he was strangely prepared to understand Jesus and to see that the true mission of the Messiah was to take up tenderly the withered flower, to plant again the fallen tree, to bind that heart that had been wounded, to raise the soul that had been bruised. That would have been John's new image of the Christ if he had been released from prison. It must surely have given to the dungeon of his closing days a light of glory which his brightest morning had never known and it must have taken from his heart every fear of death. It happens that way to a man who has been broken at his strongest point. The Christ he proclaims is the Christ whom he needs, the Christ who comes to him in pity and love. That Christ ushers him into the kingdom of God.

CHAPTER NOTES:

1. Matt. 11:11
2. Luke 1:17
3. Luke 1:43
4. Luke 1:66
5. Luke 1:76
6. Luke 3:1-17
7. Matt. 3:13-17
8. John 1:19-28
9. John 1:29-37
10. John 3:25-30
11. Matt. 11:2-19
12. Mark 6:14-29
13. Matt. 11:28 (K.J.V.)

II

These Followed Him

5
Peter

OF ALL THE men who followed Jesus during his earthly ministry the one I should most like to meet is Simon Peter. He is an interesting person, and I like interesting people. That's not to say that the other disciples are not interesting, but Peter is a special kind of person. He is so human. He never lives on the level ground but is either up in the mountain or down in the valley. He is capable of such moral extremes — stability and instability, cowardice and courage, weakness and strength, despair and hope, selfishness and love. As Simon the man of sand, he sinks to the depths of misery. As Peter, the man of rock, he rises to the heights of grandeur.

The Gospels are full of Peter. He is always on stage. He has an acting and speaking part in almost every scenario. Sometimes he plays a supporting role to Jesus, sometimes a role that lets his Master down. Peter's name always heads the list of disciples.[1] We know more about him than about any of the others. In fact, we know so much that we could easily get lost in a catalogue of facts and fail to find him as a real person. To understand his character, therefore, we shall pick out one typical incident from Peter's life with Jesus and make it the framework of the larger story.

The incident was a storm on the Sea of Galilee, one of those sudden storms where the winds sweep down from the surrounding hills and whip up waves eighteen feet high. It happened in the hours between midnight and dawn and it spelled disaster for the small fishing boat that contained the nucleus of the Christian Church. The disciples had just about prepared to meet their God when they saw something that was even more frightening than the storm — a human figure walking on the waves. "It is a ghost!" they cried out in terror. Then they saw that the "ghost" was Jesus. He spoke to them, "Take heart! It is I; do not be afraid."[2] That's where the incident became a little drama of Peter. There were three moments in it.

The First Moment

In the first moment Peter, trying to balance himself in the tossing boat, called across the waves to Jesus, "Lord, if it is you, tell me to come to you over the water." "Come", said Jesus. And Peter stepped down from the boat and walked across the water. Right away that tells us something about him. It tells us that he was not afraid of the water but was, in fact, very much at home on the water, being a fisherman by trade whom Jesus called from his fishing boats to become a fisher of men. All the Gospel writers tell the story of Peter's call.[3] They tell us that he lived in Capernaum, the busy port on the western shore of the Sea of Galilee, and that he was in the fishing business with his brother Andrew who also became a disciple of Jesus. Peter was married; and his home became a kind of headquarters for Jesus during his ministry in that city.[4] We never meet his wife or his children but we do meet his mother-in-law. We know that she lived with him, and that tells us something more about Peter.

The sea-walking incident tells us also that Peter was a leader among the disciples, a spokesman for the others. Whenever Jesus told a parable that they didn't understand, it was Peter who asked for an explanation.[5] If they had any kind of puzzlement in their minds, e.g. about the number of times you ought to forgive a person who injures you, it was Peter who articulated the question.[6] When Jesus turned away the Rich Young Ruler and sadly exclaimed that rich people will have difficulty entering the Kingdom of God, it was Peter who said what was on the minds of all the disciples, "We have left everything to become your followers...".[7] When the crowds, including many nameless disciples, deserted Jesus, because his teaching became too demanding, and he asked the Twelve, "Do you also want to leave me?" it was he asked the Twelve, "Do you also want to leave me?" it was Peter who answered with loyalty and love, "Lord, to whom shall we go? Your words are words of eternal life." The supreme example came on the road to Caeserea Philippi where Jesus asked his disciples the question that they had been asking themselves, "Who do you say that I am?" Again it was Peter who answered for all the rest, "You are the Messiah, the Son of the living God." Jesus in that moment saw that Peter was no ordinary person. We see it too. We see him as the first of the followers of Jesus to recognise the mystery of his Divine nature. No wonder the others acknowledged him as their leader.

The sea-walking incident shows Peter as an impulsive man. A cool-headed person would think twice before stepping out of a boat in the middle of a deep lake and trying to walk on the choppy water. Not Peter. He rarely thought twice. He didn't have a cool head. He responded immediately, he acted impulsively, he blurted out what was on his mind. Not one of the other disciples had exactly his temperament. John was intuitive, meditative, mystical; Philip was phlegmatic; Judas was calculating; Thomas was melancholy and morose. Peter was as sensitive as a thermometer. He was quick-tempered, emotional, enthusiastic and easily aroused by an appeal to adventure. Walking on the water was some adventure!

The sea-walking incident shows Peter to be a man of considerable courage. None of the others would have dared to trust himself to the waves. Peter didn't even notice the waves. Christ had called him, and wherever Christ called he would follow. He displayed the same courage in the Upper Room by declaring, "Everyone else may fall away but I will not"; and when Jesus predicted that Peter would deny him, he retorted stoutly, "Even if I must die with you, I will not deny you." [10] He showed courage in the Garden of Gethsemane by being the one disciple who drew a sword and tried to fight back the enemies of Jesus.[11] He displayed it again by following Jesus after his arrest to the house of the High Priest. Whatever his conduct in the courtyard, at least he was there like a lamb in a lair of lions, and that took courage.

Yes, I am attracted to Peter. I can see the rippling muscles on his back as he pulls the fishing boat toward the shore and lifts it on the beach. He has large hands and a large heart, strong shoulders and a strong personality. He is a plain, blunt, honest man. I like the boyish expression on his wind-swept face, the twinkle in his eyes and the heartiness of his laugh. He is warm, generous and outgoing. There is no question why Jesus chose him as a disciple, no question why the others looked to him as a leader, no question why Jesus, the first time they met, gave him a new name: "You are Simon, son of John. You shall be called Cephas [that is, Peter, the Rock]."[13]

The Second Moment

Now comes the second moment in the sea-walking drama, and with it comes a sudden change in Peter's character. "When he saw the strength of the gale, he was seized with fear; and beginning to sink, he cried, 'Save me, Lord!' " Why? The gale had not grown stronger. The outward situation remained the same. The change must have taken place inside Peter. Suddenly the hero became a coward, the man of rock became a man of sand. That was no isolated incident but a symbol of his whole life, a miniature of his entire character. We often see Peter on top of the waves, daring a deed that none of the others would have dared, yet a moment later shrieking with abject terror, "Save me, Lord!"

He was a coward at Caesarea Philippi. No sooner did he confess Jesus to be the Messiah and win the Master's praise for his inspired insight than he tried to divert Jesus from his appointed path of suffering and death. As none of the disciples would ever have dared to do, he took Jesus by the arm and began to rebuke him, "Heaven forbid!...this shall never happen to you." Loyalty? No. Cowardice. Peter saw very clearly, and he didn't need Jesus to tell him, that if the Messiah must go to a cross, his followers would have to join him there. A very different spirit possessed Peter in that moment, the same spirit that wrestled with Jesus and tried to compromise him in the wilderness of temptation. To that spirit in Peter Jesus again cried out, "Away with you, Satan; you are a stumbling-block to me. You think as men think, not as God thinks."[14]

Peter was a coward on the Mount of Transfiguration.[15] When he and the other two disciples saw Jesus drenched in dazzling light and flanked by Moses and Elijah, he said,

"Master, how good it is that we are here! Shall we make three shelters, one for you, one for Moses, and one for Elijah?" As though to excuse Peter, the Gospel writer adds, "but he spoke without knowing what he was saying." The chances are that Peter knew exactly what he was saying. It was comfortable and glorious on the mountain-top far above the world of suffering and hatred and violence, and Peter was saying, "We are safe in this haven of peace. Let's stay here. Let's make it permanent. Let's settle for this limited glory. Let's not go down to a cross."

In the Upper Room on the night before he was crucified Jesus predicted Peter's cowardice. [16] When that impulsive disciple bravely declared, "I am ready to go with you to prison and death," Jesus said sadly, "I tell you, Peter, the cock will not crow tonight until you have three times over denied that you know me." It was not a cynical statement, not a put-down, but a statement of fact spoken in love. With reason Jesus predicted Peter's cowardice and he told him the reason: "Simon, Simon [note the use of the old name], take heed: Satan has been given leave to sift all of you like wheat..." That is consistent with Satan's strategy. He doesn't waste time on weaklings. He tries to drag down the big men who will drag the little ones down with them. He doesn't succeed, however, because he has an adversary stronger than himself who says to Peter, "But for you I have prayed that your faith may not fail; and when you have come to yourself you must lend strength to your brothers."

Satan got to Peter outside the house of the High Priest where Jesus was on trial for his life. To be sure, it took courage for him to be in the lions' lair, but his courage quickly drained away when the lions turned on him. [17] To the innocent remark of a servant girl, "You were with Jesus," he retorted hotly, "I do not know what you mean." When another girl said to the bystanders, "This fellow was with Jesus of Nazareth," Peter swore, saying, "I do not know the man." As the bystanders closed in on him, he broke into curses, declaring with another oath, "I do not know the man." Just then the Man turned and looked at him, not with rebuke but with tenderness, as though to say, "Never mind, Peter. It's all right. I understand;" and with that look of love searing his soul and the crowing of a cock heralding the dawn of Good Friday, Peter stumbled into the darkness weeping bitterly.

There was a famous preacher in England at the turn of the century named Joseph Parker; and there was a famous theologian, with an acid tongue, named P.T. Forsyth. It is rumoured that Forsyth said about Parker, "I used to think he was a great man with a little egotism, but now I have decided that he is an egotist with a little greatness." Before going on to the third moment in the sea-walking drama let's ask about Peter — was he by nature a brave man who occasionally lost his nerve, or was he a man of extreme timidity who showed occasional flashes of courage? What do you think? The most likely answer is that he combined the two qualities in his character like two sides of a coin. Sometimes the coin fell heads and sometimes it fell tails. Let's say that his soul was a battleground between cowardice and courage. That's what made him so human and that's what brings him close to us. We can identify with Peter, we can recognise the same conflict in ourselves, a conflict never more severe than in our commitment to Jesus Christ. One moment we are ready to follow Jesus across the waves, the next moment we are terrified of sinking beneath our depth. In our Christian witness we rise to heights of grandeur and we sink to depths of misery. There is some rock and some sand in all of us.

The Third Moment

It is doubtful that Peter ever resolved the conflict. One commentator neatly divides Peter's life into three stages: (1) the time when timidity reigns supreme; (2) the stage in which there begins a struggle between timidity and a new principle — courage; (3) that period in which the new principle vanquishes the old and courage becomes the dominant note of his life.[18] However, it really didn't go like that. The truth is that Peter remained capable of both cowardice and courage to the end of his life. An old legend tells that when persecution threatened to annihilate the church in Rome, Peter, who was leader of that church, again heard the satanic voice saying, "Deny him!" Under cover of darkness he fled from the city but on the Appian Way he met the risen Christ coming in the opposite direction. "Quo Vadis, Domine?" he asked. "Where are you going, Lord?" Jesus replied, "I am going to Rome to be crucified again." Peter turned in his tracks and went back to Rome to be crucified with him.

That was the whole secret of Peter's life and it is the truth that emerges from the third moment in the sea-walking drama. As Peter, with a cry for help on his lips, began to sink beneath the waves, "Jesus at once reached out and caught hold of him, and said, 'Why did you hesitate? How little faith you have!' Then they climbed into the boat, and the wind dropped." But it really wasn't a matter of faith or of cowardice giving way to courage. It was Christ introducing a new factor into Peter's situation. "Jesus...reached out and caught hold of him." In contact with Jesus Peter became a different man. In fact, he is probably the supreme example in the New Testament of what does happen to a man in the hands of Christ. We see it all through his career.

There was the occasion of his call from a fishing boat on the Sea of Galilee, another little drama that has its own moments.[19] It began with an act of God's grace and power — a huge haul of fish that loaded two boats to the point of sinking. It was not the fish that impressed Peter but the awareness that God through Jesus had touched his life in a new and decisive way. Falling at Jesus' feet, he cried, "Go, Lord, leave me, sinner that I am!" That was not a morbid guilt or a mock humility but a recognition of the holiness and purity of Christ, a way of saying, "How can I, sinner that I am, stand in the presence of the Most High?" Jesus looked at the big fisherman with loving acceptance. "Do not be afraid," he said, "from now on you will be catching men." And Peter responded by doing what very few men have the courage to do: he left behind everything that represented his security and followed Jesus into history.

There was the occasion of the feet-washing in the Upper Room.[20] The disciples in their jealous bickering had neglected that customary courtesy among themselves, so Jesus without saying a word rose from the table, took a basin and towel and began washing their filthy feet. That embarrassed everybody. They saw that everything was the wrong way around. Jesus was Master, they were the servants. They ought to be washing his feet, not allowing him to wash theirs. As usual, it was Peter who protested, "I will never let you wash

my feet." But Jesus insists that we let him wash our feet.
Before demanding that we do anything for him he demands
that we allow him to do something for us. "If I do not wash
you, you are not in fellowship with me." Peter replied, "Not
my feet only; wash my hands and my head as well." He was
saying, in effect, "Lord, cleanse my whole personality. I need
everything from you. I cannot possibly be of any use to you
until I have accepted all that you can do for me."

The great occasion was a post-Resurrection repeat performance of the miraculous draught of fishes.[21] Peter knows
that Christ has been raised from the dead but he is not sure
what to do about it, so he goes back to Galilee and back to his
fishing boats. When the stranger standing on the beach shows
them where to catch fish, and when Peter hears John shout,
"It is the Lord!," he jumps into the water. He always seems to
be jumping out of a boat into the water. Fortunately
the water is shallow and calm this time. On the shore there
follows an amazing bit of psychotherapy as three times,
corresponding to the three denials, Christ calls Peter by the old
name and asks, "Simon, son of John, do you love me more than
all else?" He knows that Peter loves him but he makes him say
it again and again until the love that fills his heart is so
powerful that it drives out all fear and prepares him to continue
the ministry of Christ on earth. It is the sea-walking incident
again — Jesus reaching out his hand and touching Peter,
making him the man that he could never have made himself.

In his book, *Dr. Schweitzer of Lambarene*,[22] Norman Cousins
describes the regular after-dinner ritual in the jungle hospital.
He tells us that the great doctor announced the hymn to be
sung and walked over to an upright piano on the other side of
the room where he sat down to play. The piano, says Cousins,
must have been at least fifty years old. The keyboard was
badly stained. Large double screws fastened the ivory to each
note. One or more strings were missing on at least a dozen
keys. Under equatorial conditions of extreme heat and
moisture you don't even try to keep a piano in tune. And
now, one of the world's great musicians, the greatest living
interpreter of Bach's organ music, sat down to play this
dilapidated old instrument. The amazing and wondrous
thing, writes Norman Cousins, was that the piano seemed to

lose its poverty in his hands. Its tinniness and clattering echoes seemed subdued. Its capacity to yield music was now being fully realised. Whatever the reason, Schweitzer's presence at the piano seemed to make it right.

That old piano is the figure of a human character, Peter's character, your character or mine, in the hands of the Master of Life. As long as it remains sensitive to his touch, he brings out its latent qualities of love and courage, fidelity and endurance. Christ does that for Peter. He also does it for you.

CHAPTER NOTES:

1. Mark 3:16; Matt. 10:2; Luke 6:12-14
2. Matt. 14:22-33
3. Matt. 4:18-20; Mark 1:16-18; Luke 5:1-11; John 1:40-42
4. Mark 1:29-2:12
5. Matt. 15:15; Luke 12:41
6. Matt. 18:21
7. Mark 10:17-31
8. John 6:59-69
9. Matt. 16:13-20
10. Mark 14:26-31
11. John 18:1-11
12. Mark 14:66-72
13. John 1:43
14. Matt. 16:21-23
15. Luke 9:28-36
16. Luke 22:31-34
17. Matt. 26:69-73; Mark 14:66-72; Luke 22:54-61; John 18:12-27
18. George Matheson, *Representative Men of the New Testament* (Hodder and Stoughton, London, 1903), pp. 88-108
19. Luke 5:1-11
20. John 13:3ff
21. John 21:1-23
22. Harper and Brothers, New York, 1960, pp. 9-10

6
John

Two Portraits of a Man

IN THE CANADIAN School of Missions at Toronto there hangs a
pair of portraits painted in 1903 and 1904 by Dr. J.W.L.
Forster. They tell the spiritual biography of Miss Smart, a
young art student whom Dr. Forster used as a model. The
first painting, which bears the title "Perplexed", shows her
gaudily dressed in colours of green, red and gold and
surrounded by a number of pagan symbols, including a
crystal gazer's ball. She appears dejected and disillusioned
like one who has drifted into a maze of make-believe and who
desperately longs to find her way back to reality. The second
portrait, which bears the title "Faith", is so completely
different that you scarcely recognise it as representing the
same person. It shows the young student no longer surrounded by symbols but dressed in a pure white robe and looking
upwards with a serene expression on her beautiful face. Miss
Smart found what she had lost; she rediscovered her faith; by
the grace of God she stopped drifting and was brought back
again to the eternally real.

We may not have realised that there are two portraits of
the Apostle John in the New Testament and that they differ
as radically as those two portraits of the young art student.
Probably we have looked only at the second and more
familiar portrait which shows John as the disciple whom
Jesus loved and as the author of the Fourth Gospel. It is a
pleasing portrait, and we have assumed that John could have
sat for it even before he met Jesus. We assume that he was
always like that. We recognise that the other disciples had

their human weaknesses that gradually turned into strengths, but John we have judged to be a saint from the beginning.

We realise how wrong we are when we look at the first of the two portraits, the one that we have usually ignored. It is not an unattractive likeness. It cannot be so, because John was basically a good man, or Jesus would not have chosen him as a disciple. Yet the portrait does have some unattractive features. One of them is worldliness — which we can understand, because John and his twin brother, James, were fairly successful fishermen before they abandoned their boats to follow Jesus. They were not as poor as some of the other disciples. Their father, Zebedee, employed servants.[1] John had more outlets to worldly influence, including an acquaintance with the High Priest in Jerusalem.[2] On at least one occasion he seemed to emerge as a mother's darling, a spoiled and misguided boy. [3]

Yet it was not a smug worldliness, because the portrait shows also a certain discontent on the face of John. Many things suggest that he and James were a pair of radicals. Though less extreme than the fanatical Zealots, they belonged to the tribe of angry young men who wanted to upset the established order, and that may be one reason why they were willing to follow Jesus. That didn't necessarily make them any more attractive. In one of his plays Archibald MacLeish makes a character say, "Piety's hard enough to take among the poor who *have* to practise it. A rich man's piety stinks."[4] The same has been said of social radicalism. There is something incongruous about a prosperous socialist, a man who champions the cause of the underdog without seriously intending to share his kennel.

The face in the portrait wears an intolerant expression, and that also can be typical of the young radical. He has a vast reservoir of self-confidence, he doesn't like to be contradicted and he doesn't have much time for other people's views. Neither does he have a sense of humour. There are only two ways to change the world — his way and the wrong way. People either march under his flag and speak his language, or he puts them in a class with his enemies. John showed that intolerant spirit. One day he saw a man casting out devils in the name of Jesus, but the man was not a disciple, he didn't belong to the in-group, so John ordered him to stop. Jesus quietly reminded John that he and that man were both fighting on the same side.[5]

Behind the intolerant expression on the portrait we can detect a smouldering temper ready to burst into violent flame. Both sons of Zebedee had that feature, and that's why Jesus gave them the nickname, Boanerges, meaning Sons of Thunder.[6] Jesus himself had a temper that blazed out at injustice and hypocrisy. The Thunder Boys, however, like many young radicals, became angry for less mature reasons. They were ready to react with violence against personal insults. On one occasion Jesus and the disciples were refused entrance to a Samaritan village where they had expected to be hospitably received. That infuriated James and John, who remembered some of the good things that Jesus had said about Samaritans and done for them, and they proposed that Jesus retaliate by bringing down fire from heaven to destroy the village. They could almost smell the burning flesh. With amazing patience Jesus rebuked them and simply moved on to another village.[7]

The face in the portrait is an ambitious face. Like the faces of many young radicals it is the expression not of a social crusader but of an "out" who simply wants to get "in". All the disciples wanted to get in and they believed that they would get in when God's Messiah came to establish his Kingdom on earth. They thought of Jesus, in spite of all that he did and said, as a political Messiah on his way to inaugurate a political kingdom, and that made their mouths water as they thought of the political plums. One day, on the road to Jerusalem, James and John quietly approached their Master and tried to pluck two of thosee plums. "Grant us to sit in state with you, one at your right and the other at your left." That brought the other disciples running. Like animals at feeding time they milled around their Master, all scrambling for preferment and all babbling indignantly against these two opportunists who had tried to steal a march on them.[8]

The Fourth Gospel

A worldly, discontented, intolerant, hot-tempered, ambitious young radical — such is the unmistakeable portrait of John that emerges from the early part of the Gospel story. We wonder how such a man could be remembered in history as the disciple whom Jesus loved. We wonder how he could have written the Fourth Gospel, the most deeply spiritual, theological and meditative of the four Gospels, the Gospel of love, the Gospel with such power to transform human lives. I remember talking with a Bible scholar at Oxford who for many years had been planning to publish a commentary on John's Gospel. It was, in fact, published after his death under the title, *The Open Heaven*.[9] At the time he said to me, "I am not yet satisfied that I have really probed the mystery of the Fourth Gospel. I have spent a lifetime studying it, but its deepest meaning still eludes me." Then he smiled shyly and said, "You see, it isn't just an academic study. The Gospel of John means more to me than any other book in the world. It has not only changed my thinking; it has changed my life."

Some scholars say emphatically that the author of the Fourth Gospel was not the Apostle John but another John, known as "John the Presbyter" or "John the Elder", who wrote in Ephesus some sixty years after the events of Jesus' ministry. That may be true, but it is also possible that John the disciple, also living in Ephesuus, supplied the author with most of his facts. John must have had something to do with the writing of the Fourth Gospel. Apart from the long interpretative passages, it contains a wealth of factual information which was not available to Matthew, Mark or Luke and which could have come only from an eye-witness who lived very close to the historic Jesus. He alone tells of such incidents as the raising of Lazarus[10] and the appearance of the Risen Christ to Mary Magdalene in the garden.[11] He alone reports the interviews with Nicodemus[12] and the Woman of Samaria.[13] He alone gives substance to such obscure personalities as Thomas[14] and Nathaniel.[15] He alone remembers little details like the number of stone water pots[16] and the exact hour of the day.[17] The question is not whether the disciple whom Jesus loved could have written the Fourth Gospel but whether the man whose portrait we have just seen could have written it. The obvious answer to that question is No.

Look, then, at the second portrait of John which shows a
man who could have written the Fourth Gospel or who
certainly could have been the authority behind it. In many
ways it resembles the first portrait. The shape of the nose, the
colour of the eyes, the texture of the hair remain recognisable;
but the expression on the face is so different that we can
scarcely believe that the artist used the same person as a
model. The two portraits belong to different atmospheres, one
to earth and the other to heaven. This is the picture of a man
who could look back and recall that the supreme gift of Jesus
in the face of violence was a gift of peace[18] and recall that the
supreme commandment of Jesus in the teeth of hate was a
commandment to love.[19] This is the picture of a man who,
though he knew of the deceit and treachery of Judas Iscariot,
could still treat Judas as a brother.[20] This is the picture of a
man who arrived first at the Empty Tomb on Easter morning
and, with no other evidence before his eyes, saw and
believed.[21] This is a changed man. All his essential features
have changed. What brought about the change?

The Transforming Friendship

Henry Drummond concluded his famous sermon, "The
Greatest Thing in the World," by saying that if you put a
piece of iron in the presence of an electrified body, that piece
of iron for a time becomes electrified. In the presence of a
permanent magnet it is changed into a temporary magnet,
and as long as you leave the two together, they will share this
characteristic. So also, if you put a person in the presence of
Christ, he will take on the likeness of Christ and reproduce
qualities of character which by himself he could never
possibly cultivate.

For three years John lived in the magnetic presence of
Jesus. He was one of the twelve whom Jesus called to be his
companions, to share his ministry of teaching and healing
and to continue it after his death.[22] He was one of the inner
circle of three disciples with whom Jesus shared some of his
more intimate experiences — his raising of Jairus' daughter,
[23] his glory on the Mount of Transfiguration,[24] and his agony
in the Garden of Gethsemane.[25] Although Peter by his

strength of character emerged as the leader of the twelve, John by his depth of character was especially close to the mind and heart of Jesus. At the Last Supper in the Upper Room he sat in the place of honour at Jesus' right hand and received from the Master a confidence that could not have been shared with the others.[26] It is true to say that John lived closer to Jesus than any other man in history. How could he help taking on some of the qualities of Jesus?

John not only lived in friendship with Jesus, he heard the teachings of Jesus. Some were directed to the crowds, some to the disciples, and some specifically to John himself. The message came across loud and clear on the day when he and James put in their bid for the chief seats in the Kingdom of God. Jesus did not reprimand them for their ignorant self-seeking. Patiently and lovingly he expounded for their benefit the first principle of the Christian life. He reminded them that in the kingdoms of the world the standard of greatness is power, and a man is counted great according to the number of people he controls and the measure of service he can command. The world sees greatness as a pyramid, and the great man is the man who sits on top. Then he told John that in the Kingdom of God the standard of greatness is love, and a man is counted great according to the number of people he helps and the measure of service he can give. Thus the pyramid is inverted, so that the nearer a man gets to the peak, the lower his prestige, the heavier his burden, and the more people he carries in love.[27] For John that teaching must have been like the smashing of a mirror. It must have turned his life upside down. How could he ever be the same again?

John not only heard the teaching of Jesus, he saw the example of Jesus whose whole life illustrated the concept of true greatness, "Whoever wants to be great must be your servant, and whoever wants to be first must be the willing slave of all. For even the Son of Man did not come to be served but to serve, and to surrender his life as a ransom for many."[28] That came to a climax on the Cross where Jesus did, in fact, surrender his life as a ransom for many. Yet even before the Cross John saw the servant concept in action, especially in the Upper Room. An unemotional man, who watched the Oberammergau Passion Play, said that he remained unmoved until the scene of the feet-washing; then he felt his eyes fill with tears. John's eyes must have filled with tears when he felt the soothing hands of Jesus washing the dirt from his tired, aching feet.[29] Peter protested indignantly, Judas must have been ashamed or angry, but John must have been too choked up to speak. Not the act itself but what it symbolised broke open his heart. In the ancient world feet-washing was the menial, rather repulsive task of a slave; and Jesus, the Master, deliberately cast himself in the role of a slave. That must have affected John profoundly.

What really changed John was his particular personal experience of the love of Jesus. Scholars insist that John could not have written the Fourth Gospel in its finished form simply because it refers to him several times as "the disciple whom Jesus loved", and he would never be so conceited as to refer to himself in that way. Perhaps not. Nevertheless there is reason to suppose that, while Jesus loved all the disciples, John did have a special place in his Master's affections. It was to John alone that he spoke in his dying moments from the Cross, to John that he entrusted the care of the one person whom he held most dear on earth — his mother. The story reads: "Jesus saw his mother, with the disciple whom he loved standing beside her. He said to her, 'Mother, there is your son'; and to the disciple, 'There is your mother'; and from that moment the disciple took her into his home."[30] To the end of her life Mary would be a reminder to John that Jesus loved him, believed in him and trusted him more than he had ever dared to dream.

The Means of Grace

Those were the transforming factors in John's experience and they account for the striking contrast in the two New Testament portraits of him. They are still the transforming factors in the experience of any Christian and they are still available. We call them "the means of grace" — which implies that a transformation of character such as happened to John is not something that we can effect within ourselves. It is something which God alone by his grace can effect within us as we open our lives to the means which he has provided.

One of them is prayer. Through prayer we have friendship with God's Christ as John had friendship with him during the days of his flesh. Too often we think of prayer as a begging for favours. In fact, we don't usually pray unless we have a favour to ask. Therefore we miss the most important feature of prayer which is simply to be in the presence of Christ, asking nothing, confessing nothing, saying nothing, just being with him. Prayer, which is communion with Christ, need not be confined to special times and places; it is not an isolated act but a posture, a continual, conscious openness to the presence of Christ in all our activities and relationships. Then it becomes a transforming power in our lives.

Another means of grace is the Bible. That truth is bound up with all that John, in the opening verses of his Gospel, meant by "the Word of God", the eternal mind and reason of God, the self-communication of God that became not only audible but visible in Jesus.[31] Jesus was the Word of God made flesh; and because the words of the Bible witness to Jesus they too become the Word of God. They become like a window through which we can see Jesus, they become a mouth-piece through which Jesus can speak to us and teach us as he taught John. Those teachings are not outdated but are as capable of being practised today as they were in the days of his flesh. Any one of them, e.g., the servant-concept of greatness, contains more potential for social change than all the political systems and all the revolutionary armies put together. It will certainly turn a human life upside down.

Corporate worship is a means of grace. Some Christians neglect it, saying that they come closer to God in solitude; but the truth is that something happens in the fellowship of other believers that does not happen in solitude. Jesus said, "For where two or three have met together in my name, I am there among them."[32] One thing that happens in the fellowship of Christians is that you look beyond yourself and see, as John saw, the example of Jesus. Where else but the Church do you see an example like that of Cardinal Leger, Archbishop of Montreal, the largest Roman Catholic Diocese in the world, who abdicated his role as a prince of the Church and went to work among the lepers in Africa as a missionary priest? He said that he did so because he wanted to be at the bottom of the pyramid, not the top; he wanted to serve and not be served. It was a Christly thing to do and it had a powerful impact on the consciences of many other Christians.

The distinctively Christian means of grace is the Sacrament of Holy Communion. Churches differ in their understanding of what happens at the sacramental table but they find common ground in their understanding of the word "sacramentum" which literally means "pledge". The outward symbols of bread and wine are the pledge of God's love and trust, just as the outward symbol of a wedding ring is the pledge of human love and trust. The Lord's Table does more than pledge the love of God; it dramatises that love before our eyes. The words, "This is my body...this is my blood", re-enact the Cross on which Christ's body and blood were broken and shed to demonstrate God's love for the whole world.[33] Whatever else the Lord's Table means to us, it is the one place in all the world which tells us that we are known by God, accepted by God, loved by God. Once we have gone there in faith, once we have surrendered ourselves to the transforming love of God in Christ, we can never be the same again.

Those were the factors that not only transformed John but inspired him to write his glorious Gospel with its magnificent proclamation — "the Word became flesh".[34] They are still the factors that inspire the writing of a Gospel. Live close to God's Christ in prayer, let him teach you through the Bible, see the example of his life in the fellowship of believers, experience his love in Holy Sacrament, and you also will write a Gospel, not in paper and print but in human deeds and character. The Word of God will become flesh in your life.

CHAPTER NOTES:

1. Mark 1:9-20
2. John 18:15
3. Matt. 20:20ff.
4. Archibald MacLeish,
   J.B. (Houghton
   Mifflin Company,
   Boston, 1956) p. 46
5. Luke 9:49-50
6. Mark 3:17
7. Luke 9:51-56
8. Mark 10:35ff.
9. W.H. Cadman, *The
   Open Heaven,* ed.
   George Caird (Basil
   Blackwell, Oxford 1968)
10. John 11:1ff.
11. John 20:1ff.
12. John 3:1ff.
13. John 4:1ff.
14. John 11:16;14:5;
    20:19-29
15. John 1:43-51
16. John 2:6
17. John 4:52
18. John 14:27
19. John 13:34
20. John 13:26
21. John 20:8
22. Mark 3:13-19
23. Luke 8:51
24. Mark 9:2ff.
25. Mark 4:32ff.
26. John 13:21ff.
27. Mark 10:41ff.
28. Mark 10:45
29. John 13:2ff.
30. John 19:26-27
31. John 1:1ff.
32. Matt. 18:20
33. 1 Cor. 11:26
34. John 1:14

7
Matthew

The Surprising Choice

"Jesus saw a man named Matthew at his seat in the custom-house, and said to him, 'Follow me'; and Matthew rose and followed him."[1] There are two surprising things about that encounter. First, we are surprised that Jesus said "Follow me" to a man like Matthew. That's not because of anything we know about Matthew. We know nothing about him personally. He is one of those characters in the Gospel drama, one of the disciples of Jesus, who never really emerges as a distinct personality. We do, however, know something about the kind of man that he was.

It says so in the Gospel that bears his name — "Jesus saw a man named Matthew at his seat in the custom-house..." Right away we are tempted to have some unkind thoughts about customs men, perhaps because they awaken within us a suppressed sense of guilt. I have always had the feeling, which is probably quite mistaken, that basically they are unhappy people. I have often wondered if the civil service seeks out its most miserable employees, perhaps those who are going through some kind of marital problems, and appoints them to the customs department. That's the impression you get when you encounter them at an airport or a border. Even if you have nothing to declare, the very sight of the customs officer and the way that he glares at you makes you feel like an incipient smuggler. He is probably a pleasant person in his private life, a loving father and a Boy Scout leader, but when he puts on that uniform and gets inside his little booth he begins to look like your enemy.

That's what Matthew did for a living. He was a customs officer who worked from a little toll booth by the Sea of Galilee where he collected taxes for the government. We think that taxes are something new because they have been multiplied so crazily during our lifetime. It is difficult to believe that less than a century ago William Ewart Gladstone actually opposed the imposition of income tax amounting to a penny a year on each British citizen. Gladstone should be living today when all levels of government line up like animals at a trough to take their bites out of your disposable incomes.

Today's taxes are nothing compared to those that the ancient Jews had to pay; and they chafed under them more than we do, because of all nations in the world the Jews most vigorously hated taxes. The strict Jew believed that he should pay tribute only to God, and it galled him that he had to pay tribute and so much tribute to Caesar. He paid taxes, as we do, for such benefits as highways and police protection. The amount was statutory and it offered little room for extortion and abuse. William Barclay[2] reminds us that the first century Jew had to pay also a number of occasional taxes that were not only expensive but irritating and degrading. He paid a purchase tax on all that he bought and sold, bridge money for crossing a bridge, a tax for using a road, a tax on his cart and wheels, on its axle and on the beast that drew the cart. The collector of those hated taxes was an amalgam of customs officer, bailiff and collector for a finance company. He could stop a man anywhere and demand to see his goods. He could strip off his clothes or force him to pay an impossible sum of money, then offer to lend him the money at an exorbitant rate of interest.

What kind of person would take on that job? To begin with, he had to be a man without a shred of patriotism, and that made him a rare creature among the Jews who were very patriotic. A Jew identified his country with his own soul and made its preservation his main motive for living. He could cease to love his country only by ceasing to love himself. A customs officer not only did not love his country, he exploited and looted his country and he did so out of sheer greed. The fastest way for any Jew to make money in ancient Palestine was to attach himself to the conquerers of his country and collect their tribute from his own people. He had to be a particularly despicable kind of person to do it. In Norway during the Second World War a despicable man named Quisling worked hand-in-glove with the Nazis; and since that time his name has become a synonym for all traitors. Matthew was a "quisling" — the last man on earth whom you would expect Jesus to have chosen as a disciple.

A customs officer had to be crooked. An honest man couldn't survive in the business any more than he could survive today in the prostitution or gambling rackets. He didn't get any salary from the Roman government; he probably bought his job from the government and paid for the privilege of collecting taxes. Things haven't changed all that much. Just a year ago the newspapers carried stories of some toll collectors operating on North American highways who paid as much as a thousand dollars for their jobs. They get it back with interest by slipping some of the toll fees into their own pockets. They bilk the government. Matthew bilked his customers. He added his commission to what he charged them, and sometimes the commission was bigger than the tax. He was an extortioner, he lived by rake-offs. Surely he was the last man whom you would expect Jesus to choose as a disciple.

A customs officer had to be heartless, otherwise he had better not work in a toll booth. It was no place for any man with a grain of human sympathy. I knew an admirable young man who worked for a finance company. Among other things he had to repossess goods and appliances from people who couldn't keep up the payments with their extortionate rates of interest. One day he went to his boss and said simply, "I quit. I can't do this sort of thing any more." Matthew did it all the time; it was his business. People paid up or they paid the penalty, and Matthew had to penalise them without being squeamish about it. It has been suggested that Jesus, when he was village carpenter of Nazareth, used to go over to Matthew's toll booth in Capernaum to pay his mother's taxes. Perhaps he heard the heartless customs officer threatening his victims and heard the cries of the poor as they pleaded for pity. Perhaps more than once he signed his own name to a note for this or that poor neighbour. It is possible that Jesus knew Matthew quite well — the last man in the world whom you would expect him to have chosen as a disciple.

Needless to say, customs officers and tax collectors were the most hated members of Jewish society; not only hated but ostracised and cast out from Jewish society. People treated them like moral lepers and denied them all the privileges of citizens. They were not permitted to serve either as judges or as witnesses. They were refused entrance to the synagogue. They were regarded as criminals. They had no friends except among other crooked characters like themselves, and those were not friends but partners in crime. Decent people would not associate with them, and a religious teacher would not be found talking to them. Surely Matthew was the last man whom you would expect Jesus to choose as a disciple.

Matthew's given name was Levi, and it's ironic that a person with that name should be found in the seat of corruption. Levi in the Old Testament was the tribe set apart for the service of God in the sanctuary. He was to have no possessions, because "the Lord is his inheritance."[3] But here is a Levi who is all out for material possessions and cares little for his Divine heritage. This Levi is a living contradiction of his name. He is the very embodiment of that grim picture in the Book of Malachi of the mercenary sons of Levi who have so corrupted their covenant with God that he has cursed them and made them utterly "despised and abased before all the people."[4] He is a blasphemer and surely the last man whom you would expect Jesus to choose as a disciple.

Yet Jesus called Levi and not only called him but probably gave him the new name Matthew which means "the gift of God". One day he went to the toll booth by the Sea of Galilee, where he had often gone with his mother's taxes, and looked straight at this sour-faced, crooked, quisling blasphemer whom nobody loved, and when Matthew asked, "Anything to declare?" Jesus said, "Yes, follow me."

Jesus did more than that. After spending a whole night in prayer he chose twelve disciples to be the nucleus of his Church, and Matthew was among them, the seventh in the list. Only in the Gospel that bears his name is he designated as "Matthew the tax-gatherer".[5] The other Gospels do not

list him with that stigma. We are still surprised that Jesus
included him. In fact, if Jesus, before choosing the twelve,
had shown us the list and asked for our advice, we should
probably have crossed off the name of Matthew. We can find
some reason for choosing any of the others, even Judas, but
Matthew we regard as the most unlikely candidate. Nothing
is more surprising than that Jesus should say to him, "Follow
me."

Yet is it so surprising? Does it not simply illustrate that we
have our standards and Christ has his? We look at a person
like the Rich Young Ruler, who kept the moral law from the
days of his youth,[6] and we decide that he would make an
ideal disciple. We look at Matthew, who broke the moral law
from the days of his youth, and we decide that he would not
make a disciple at all. "No," says Jesus. "It is the other way
around. Matthew will do for me what the Rich Young Ruler
will never do. He is not a bad man. He makes his living in a
bad way, but don't hold that against him. Don't identify him
with his profession. I see things about Matthew that you don't
see. I know that beneath his corrupt exterior he has a
potential for goodness. You just give him to me for a few
months, and I will show you that he is the kind of man I
need. Besides, I like the fellow in spite of the life that he has
been living for years. That's why I say to him, 'Follow me'."

The Surprising Response

There are two surprising things in the encounter beside the
Sea of Galilee. The first is that Jesus approached Matthew
and said, "Follow me." The second is that Matthew rose up
and followed him. The author of Luke's Gospel says that he
"rose to his feet, left everything behind and followed
him"[7] — which was exactly what the Rich Young Ruler
refused to do. With everything going for him morally, the
Rich Young Ruler still could not make the one response that
Jesus required. Yet here was Matthew, also a rich man but
with nothing going for him morally, who responded to Jesus
immediately and completely. We can picture him leaving his
account of unpaid taxes on the shelf, stepping outside the toll
booth, locking the door, turning his back forever on his means

of livelihood and joining the ranks of a penniless preacher. We can picture it but how shall we explain it?

Perhaps Matthew was not as ill-prepared as we imagine. Perhaps Jesus somehow got to him in those early days when he brought his mother's taxes. Maybe Matthew never felt quite right after he had taken money from those strong carpenter's hands and been searched by those pure, piercing eyes. Maybe Matthew, sitting by the shore of the lake where Jesus often preached, had caught some of the words of eternal life that fell from the Master's lips and had been subtly changed by them until now he was like a fruit ripe for the picking. Perhaps Jesus knew that Matthew would rise up and follow him, though we are still surprised by the immediacy and completeness of his response.

If Jesus had reasons for not calling Matthew, it is equally true that Matthew had reasons for not following him. We don't have to guess what they were, because they are the very reasons that still prevent people from responding to the religion of Jesus. A man will say, "I don't go to Church because I am not spiritual enough. I am not the religious type. Religion is not my thing. I have no room for it in my busy life." Another man will say, "I am not good enough to be a follower of Jesus and I don't want to try. I don't want to be obligated to lead the kind of life that a Christian is supposed to lead." Another will say, "I am not gifted enough. I don't have much education or influence. I am an ordinary person. What can I give or do for the cause of Jesus Christ?" Another will say, "I am not sure enough. There are too many beliefs in Christianity that I still don't understand. In fact, I don't know what I believe. So why be hypocritical about it?" Matthew could have thrown any or all of those reasons in the face of Christ, and it's surprising that he didn't do so. He could have said, "Go away, Jesus of Nazareth. I am not spiritual enough, not good enough, not gifted enough, not sure enough to be one of your followers. Leave me in my toll booth!"

If Matthew, the crooked customs officer, had said that, he would have missed the biggest rake-off of his life. He would have missed the greatest friendship that any man on this earth can ever experience — friendship with God's Christ.

When Jesus walked by the toll booth, Matthew didn't have a friend in the whole world. When Matthew left his toll booth, Jesus went home to eat with him; and to share a meal in the East is a pledge of mutual support and loyalty, a sacred bond of friendship. That's what scandalised the Pharisees, the respectable people, the watchdogs of religious orthodoxy. When they saw Jesus entering Matthew's house they reacted as if he were entering a brothel and indignantly asked the disciples, "Why is it that your master eats with tax-gatherers and sinners?" Jesus overheard them and said, in effect, "I eat with these people because they are the ones that need me. They have no friends, they feel rejected by God and man. They are sick and they can never be made well until they know that they are accepted. They need to recover dignity and self-respect. I give it to them in my friendship." [8]

If Matthew had stayed in his toll booth he would have missed not only the greatest friendship but also the greatest opportunity that any man on this earth can ever experience — an opportunity to play a supporting role in the redemptive drama of Christ. Playing that role became the supreme purpose of his life. It brought him to life, harnessed his energies, fulfilled his ambitions, developed his potential. It made him a real person and a whole person. To be sure, Matthew as an individual does not appear prominently in the Gospel drama. He melts into the larger apostolic group, but don't be misled by that. The supreme fact about Matthew is that one of the four Gospels, the one that appears first in the New Testament, bears his name. That suggests that he didn't leave everything belonging to his old occupation behind when he closed the door of his toll booth. He took his writing materials with him and used them in the service of Christ.

Most scholars agree that Matthew, the disciple whom Jesus called, did not write the first Gospel exactly as it stands. The fact that it bears his name, however, suggests that he may have been the authority behind it. He may have provided the author with much of his material, so that the author was saying, in effect, "Here is the story of Jesus *according to* Matthew." It seems reasonable that Matthew, the former customs officer with his capacity for keeping accurate records, kept some kind of a record of his life with Jesus. It seems reasonable that he wrote down and collected and arranged and edited many of the sayings of Jesus, the parables and pithy teachings, as he heard them. The Gospel according to Matthew portrays Jesus primarily as a teacher. Significantly enough, it is the most patriotic of the Gospels, the one that insists that Jesus, the hundred per cent Jew by lineage, birth and upbringing, was the long-awaited Messiah of Israel, foretold by the prophets. He is a teaching Messiah, not a political Messiah. He teaches men how God wants them to live in their personal and corporate lives. That's what gives Matthew's Gospel its peculiar power.

In his book, *Opium of the People*, Michael Bourdeaux shows an example of that power. He is a Church of England priest who spent several periods in the Soviet Union, including a year of graduate study at Moscow University. He says that he found it difficult to establish friendly relations with the Russian students. They were anti-religious, they had been indoctrinated against every kind of Western influence and they were afraid to be seen talking with him. Nevertheless, he was invited one evening to the apartment of a young couple who surprised him by showing him a collection of Western jazz records, including some of the latest hit tunes. They told him that they were interested in the choral music of the great masters and specified Beethoven's *Missa Solemnis* as their favourite. The young woman said, "I believe it's the piece of music where the creative mind of man reaches out furthest to God." Mr. Bourdeaux presumed that they must be speaking figuratively of God, but the young man interjected, "Not a bit of it. I was converted to Christianity in my last year at university, and my wife came to share my conviction just after we were married."

It seemed incredible to Michael Bourdeaux that under the Soviet system anyone could be converted to Christianity while still a student — and in the last year of Stalin's life, too. The young man said that actually his conversion took place a couple of months before Stalin died and he told how it happened. He said that during his first year at university he came to think of Communism as an inhuman and intolerable system. He came to religion as a matter of intellectual curiosity, thinking that there must be something in it to make it worth opposing so violently. Then, quite by accident, he struck up a friendship with a theological student who impressed him with his quiet sincerity. They met regularly, and one day the student brought him a manuscript copy of Matthew's Gospel. The young man read it carefully and was most impressed by its ethical content. He said to Mr. Bourdeaux, "It soon became obvious to me that I had discovered something here which was of infinitely greater value than any of the tomes of Marx, Engels, Lenin or Stalin which I had been forced to read at the university." He said that as a result of reading and pondering Matthew's Gospel he went to a church secretly one evening and was baptised a Christian.[9]

That incident would never have happened except that one day Jesus "saw a man named Matthew at his seat in the custom-house, and said to him, 'Follow me'; and Matthew rose and followed him." When a man says "Yes" to the call of Christ and gives Christ the obedience that he commands, he never knows what consequences might be set in motion. Matthew's Gospel presents Jesus as the King of all life and his teachings as the royal laws of his Kingdom. Matthew himself shows us that when we give Christ the sovereignty over our lives we realise our potential and fulfil our destiny as sons of God.

CHAPTER NOTES:

1. Matt. 9:9
2. Wiliam Barclay, *The Master's Men* (Abingdon Press, New York, Nashville, 1959) p. 15ff.
3. Deuteronomy 8:9 (R.S.V.)
4. Malachi 2:8-9 (R.S.V.)
5. Matt. 10:2-4
6. Mark 10:17-22
7. Luke 5:28
8. Matt. 9:10-13
9. Faber and Faber Ltd., London, 1965, pp. 148-150

8
Thomas

The Doubting Disciple

MANY PEOPLE TODAY, if they were asked to identify with one
of the disciples of Jesus, would choose Thomas — the man
who doubted and dared to express his doubts that Jesus rose
from the dead. On the evening of the first Easter Day the
Risen Christ came to his sorrowing disciples in the Upper
Room, showed them the wounds in his hands and side,
pronounced the familiar blessing, "Peace be with you", spoke
to them of their responsibilities in the world and breathed on
them his Holy Spirit. With superb understatement the Gospel
writer tells us, "Then the disciples were glad when they saw
the Lord" (R.S.V.). The New English Bible comes closer to
their mood by saying, "they were filled with joy." [1]

For some reason Thomas was not among them, so he
missed the victorious visit that turned their sorrow into joy.
Later that night he arrived on the scene and found the others
delirious with excitement but, when they told him the cause
of their excitement, "We have seen the Lord", he refused to
believe them, all ten of them. Even the ecstasy on their faces
failed to convince him. Instead of shouting for joy at the good
news of the Resurrection, Thomas sadly shook his head and
exclaimed, in effect, "I'll believe it when I see it." He actually
said, "Unless I see the mark of the nails on his hands, unless I
put my finger in the place where the nails were, and my hand
into his side, I will not believe it." [2]

That's why many people, inside and outside the churches,
are eager to identify with Thomas. They believe that they
would have reacted in the same way. Thomas mirrors their

scepticism not only about the Resurrection but about all the great doctrines of the Faith. They also want visible proof that Jesus rose from the dead. Conditioned by the secular culture, they react to any religious dogmatism by saying, "Unless I see... I will not believe." They might not have said that fifty years ago but they say it now. Doubt has become their orthodoxy, and doubting Thomas has become their patron saint. They identify with Thomas, they recognise him as the supreme realist among the disciples, they remember him preeminently as the man who doubted.

Thomas himself might not wish to be remembered in exactly that way. We can imagine him saying, "Please don't judge me only on the basis of my doubt in the Upper Room." Thomas had to be more than a man of doubt, else his name would not be listed among the original twelve disciples. The really important thing about Thomas is that Jesus, after spending a whole night in prayer, included him among the men whom he chose to share his ministry and carry it on after his death.[3] For three years he lived close to Jesus, felt the impact of the Master's personality, heard his teachings, witnessed his miracles and received his instructions. He went out on the first apostolic mission, he preached the Gospel and cast out devils and cured the sick. He was at the Last Supper and in the Garden of Gethsemane. Jesus washed his feet. Surely it is not fair to enclose Thomas' whole spiritual history in one tiny capsule of doubt.

Perhaps not, but it is possible that Thomas' doubt in the Upper Room may give us the clearest clue to his character. It couldn't have been an ordinary doubt. There had to be something special about it, or Jesus would not have treated it so leniently. Normally Jesus had no patience with the "Unless I see... I will not believe" syndrome. He refused to give the Pharisees the physical sign which they desired.[4] Yet he gave a physical sign to Thomas. On the Sunday after Easter, when the eleven disciples, Thomas included, were gathered in the same Upper Room, the Risen Christ made a second appearance presumably for Thomas' benefit. Only the two of them spoke. Jesus showed him the evidence that his eyes and hands required; and Thomas, convinced beyond all shadow of doubt, fell at his Master's feet and cried out, "My Lord and my God!"[5] That was one of the most gracious things that Jesus ever did, and there had to be a reason for it. There had to be something special about Thomas' doubt, a quality or several qualities that not only throws light on his character but also shows us where we can identify with his total experience.

Emotional Doubt

To begin with, we can say that Thomas' doubt was an emotional doubt. It rose not from the surface of his mind but from the depth of his soul. Perhaps we have put him down as an intellectual snob or at least as an urbane sceptic, the sort of man who reasonably demands that a proposition be proved before he will accept it. There are plenty of people like that. It's not that they refuse to be convinced, simply that they need to be convinced. They do not deny the reality of religious truth but they do demand that it be measured by the same tests that we apply to all other truth. Such a person would naturally doubt that anyone crucified, dead and buried, his body sealed in a rock-hewn tomb, could possibly be walking about the earth three days after he had been pronounced dead. Such a doubter we may have imagined Thomas to be.

We get a different picture by reading the New Testament and piecing together what little information we can find about Thomas. There was nothing urbane about him, nothing to suggest that he was better educated than the other disciples. All we know with any certainty about his mental equipment is that he was a confirmed pessimist who always looked on the dark side of things. When Jesus announced his intention to leave Galilee and go to Jerusalem, Thomas was quite sure that it meant death for all of them.[6] When Jesus on the eve of his Crucifixion spoke comforting words about going to other rooms in his Father's house, Thomas broke in with the sad and hopeless protest, "Lord, we do not know where you are going, so how can we know the way?" He received a great answer from Jesus: "I am the way; I am the truth and I am life; no one comes to the Father except by me."[7]

The great answer may have satisfied his mind but it did

not satisfy his emotions. Some men are melancholy because they are sceptical. Thomas was sceptical because he was melancholy. His melancholy reached its lowest depth on Golgotha. The sight of Jesus hanging on the Cross struck a mortal blow to every hope he had ever cherished in his gloomy heart. Neither his recollection of Jesus' promise nor the radiant good news that his Master had returned from the dead could retrieve Thomas from the abyss of despondency and gloom. His was not the doubt of reasoned argument but the doubt of deep despair.

That is why the Risen Christ came to Thomas and dispelled his doubts. God may leave us to resolve our intellectual doubts by ourselves but he comes to our help in the deeper doubt of emotional despair. It is not generally known that the two Scottish theologians, John and Donald Baillie, had a younger brother, Peter. Their mother, twice widowed in early life, worked and struggled and saved and prayed to put her sons through Edinburgh University. John and Donald became ordained ministers of high distinction. Peter graduated in medicine and sailed for India as a medical missionary. To Mrs. Baillie it seemed that all the years of struggle had been worthwhile. Then came the stunning blow. Peter, still at language school, died in a drowning accident even before he could begin his missionary career. That was too much for his mother. Strong saint as she was, the tragedy shattered her faith in the God whom she had always trusted and served. But God did not leave her in the misery of doubt. Her sons, John and Donald, tenderly nursed her back to a merciful faith in loving Providence. Christ came again to his doubting disciple, as he came to Thomas in the Upper Room, so that with Thomas she could cry out, "My Lord and my God!" [8]

Anguished Doubt

We notice also that Thomas' doubt was an anguished doubt. The story is told that when Benjamin Jowett was Master of Balliol College, Oxford, an undergraduate came to him one day and said jauntily, "I am having difficulty finding proof for the existence of God." Jowett snapped, "Well, young man, you had better find God before five

o'clock this afternoon, or you will have to leave this college."
Flippant doubt, that never sheds a tear in its assumed
intellectual superiority, deserves to be dealt with in exactly
that way. The French philosopher Pascal once wrote, "I have
nothing but compassion for all who sincerely lament their
doubt, who look upon it as the worst of all evils and spare no
pains to escape it; but if this condition of doubt forms the
subject of a man's joy and boasting, I have no terms in which
to describe a creature so extravagant."

There was nothing flippant about Thomas' doubt. It made
him miserable. We can guess why he was absent from the
Upper Room on the evening of Easter Day. When he saw the
body of his Lord laid in the tomb, dark night settled upon his
soul, and he wanted to be alone. Like a well-bred animal,
when it is injured, he crept away to suffer by himself. He had
nothing but grief in his heart, and the company of others
would only aggravate his grief. Do you think that it pleased
him later to tell his friends that they were the victims of an
hallucination? When Thomas lost his Lord he lost everything,
and having to doubt the good news of the Resurrection only
deepened his melancholy and made him unspeakably more
wretched.

Doubt does have the power to make us wretched. A fine
Christian lady burst out bitterly, "I think I must be an
atheist!" She had always been a religious person, always
attended church, always believed what Christians are supposed to believe; but now for the first time in her life the cold
fingers of doubt gripped her heart, and she found herself
questioning the Faith that she had taken for granted since
childhood. It was an anguished doubt. It chilled her soul like
a spiritual disease, and she felt ashamed and guilty and
frightened lest she communicate it to her husband and her
growing boys. In sheer desperation she confided to a close
friend, "I still go to church, I try to keep up appearances, but
I just can't be sure any more. It's a terrible thing to lose your
religious faith!"

There are two kinds of anguished doubt. There is the
anguish of the sincere agnostic — not the dogmatic atheist
but the sincere agnostic — who feels a deep and passionate
need to believe but simply cannot bring himself to believe.

This mood of yearning and searching and reaching out, which runs through much of our modern culture, is a tragic and shattering frame of mind, even though it may give birth to an infant faith. There is also the anguish of having lost a full-grown faith, the misery of not being sure where once you were sure, of walking in the shadows where once you walked in the sunlight. The great believers have all known this dark night of the soul, because the greater a man's faith, the more vulnerable he is to doubt. The darkness is terrible while it lasts but the darkness will pass, and Christ will come to his anguished servant as he came to Thomas, so that with Thomas he can cry out, "My Lord and my God!"

Honest Doubt

Thomas' doubt was also an honest doubt. There was nothing faked about it. To the other disciples he said stubbornly, "Unless I see… I will not believe," but to God he must have cried out from the depths of pessimism and melancholy, "I pray that I *shall* see. I pray that this incredible good news of the Master's Resurrection, which to my reason sounds fantastic and hopeless, is actually true." Thomas passionately longed to see his Lord again. He would have given anything to be certain that Jesus was not dead but alive. He really wanted to believe.

One gets the impression that some doubters do not want to believe. They have nothing in common with Thomas, nothing in common with the sincere agnostics. They worship their own arguments. If someone, who has thought and lived more deeply than they, exploded their arguments, they would promptly construct a new set of doubts to replace the old. Complacently they quote the familiar lines of Tennyson, "There lives more faith in honest doubt…than in half the creeds", but there is nothing honest about their doubt, nothing original. It has been plagiarised from magazines and borrowed from spiritually bankrupt broadcasters. Were they really honest, they would at least do justice to Tennyson and recall that the lines are taken from his poem, "In Memoriam", which is one of the sublimest expressions of faith in English literature:

Strong Son of God, Immortal Love,
Whom we, that have not seen Thy face,
By faith and faith alone embrace,
Believing where we cannot prove.

Because he doubted honestly Thomas stuck close to the other disciples. He had abandoned them after the dreadful events of the Crucifixion. Why not again after judging that they had all taken leave of their senses? Everything suggests that he really wanted to believe their fantastic story about Christ rising from the dead and appearing to them in the Upper Room. We can imagine him fairly pestering them, one after the other, with questions, begging them to rehearse every detail of the Divine visitation, hoping against hope that their confident witness would finally overcome his doubts and convince him of the truth.

That was a sensible thing to do. The honest doubter, if he has lost Christ and wants to find him again, will stick closer than ever to the community of believing Christians. Arthur John Gossip, the Scottish preacher, declared from the depths of personal tragedy, "Some people, when belief comes hard, fling away from the Christian faith altogether." Then he asked, "In heaven's name, fling away to what?" The torment of doubt is no time to divorce ourselves from the fellowship and the resources of religious faith, no time to stop praying and throw away the Bible and turn our backs on the Church. Doubts torment us, not because we have too much religion but because we have too little. We shall prove the honesty of our doubt by the earnestness of our efforts to resolve it; and, if we are honest, our efforts will be rewarded, and Christ will come to us as he came to Thomas, so that we also may cry out, "My Lord and my God!"

Loyal Doubt

Most important of all, Thomas' doubt was a loyal doubt. We can be sure of that because of what we know about him. The other disciples may have been quicker than he to understand and believe Jesus, but he followed Jesus on the basis of what he *could* understand and believe. He may have been pessimistic, melancholy and doubtful but he was never disloyal. He never allowed doubt to interfere with duty. When Jesus announced his intention to go up to Jerusalem, not only Thomas but all the disciples knew that it was like walking into a death-trap and they voted unanimously against it. Well, not quite unanimously. One heroic spirit stood out against the others. One man spoke words of unfaltering fidelity. Thomas could not deflect his Master from the road to Calvary, nor could he understand why that road must be travelled, but at least he would not allow his Master, whom he loved more than life, to walk it alone. To the others he said, "Let us also go, that we may die with him."[9]

There is one variety of doubt that God will never dispel. It is the doubt that becomes an easy and shallow escape from the moral obligations and disciplines of religion. A person will say, "I am not an atheist. I do not deny the existence of God. But there are too many questions that have not yet been answered to my satisfaction, questions about the Virgin Birth and the Trinity and the Resurrection and other dogmas in the Apostles' Creed. Therefore I cannot become a Christian." That could be a sincere doubt or it could be the doubt of a troubled conscience. If such a person came to terms with the Ten Commandments he might have less difficulty with the Apostles' Creed. One is always tempted to ask him, "If all those questions were answered to your satisfaction, would you then become a Christian? Would you accept Jesus Christ as the Lord of your life and give him your undivided loyalty and obedience? That's what it means to be a Christian."

In a book called *Life is Commitment* the author, J.H. Oldham, has written, "There are some things in life — and they may be the most important things — that we cannot know by research or reflection, but only by committing ourselves. We must dare in order to know."[10] That is supremely true of the great doctrines of the Christian religion. Like stained glass windows they cannot be clearly seen and appreciated from outside but only from inside the structure of faith. It is especially true of the Resurrection. The Risen Christ did not appear to his enemies or even to his casual friends; they would not have recognised him. He appeared to his disciples, the men and women who had followed him and obeyed his teachings and were committed to his way of life. They dared in order to know. That is the only requisite of faith and the only answer to doubt.

So it happened to Thomas on the Sunday after Easter. Christ came to this loyal doubter and gave him the visible proof that he had risen from the dead and was eternally alive. The man who doubts as a mental exercise, who secretly enjoys doubting, who doesn't really want to believe and who makes his doubts an excuse for moral and spiritual laziness — that man will forever stumble in the darkness of unbelief. But he who doubts sincerely, sorrowfully, honestly, longing for certitude and meanwhile following such flickering light as he has — that man will some day emerge into the bright sunlight of a full, mature Christian faith. To that man Christ will reveal himself more and more, until one day he cries out with Thomas, "My Lord and my God!"

Then why did Jesus rebuke Thomas? Why did he seem to throw cold water over his disciple's ecstasy by saying, "Because you have seen me you have found faith. Happy are they who never saw me and yet have found faith"? [11] Obviously Thomas must learn that true faith does not demand visible proof. True faith believes where it cannot prove and brings the greater happiness. Because he *saw* the Risen Christ Thomas could cry out, "My Lord and my God!" but it was another disciple who proclaimed the highest praise of the Risen Christ when he later wrote to Christians far away, "Without having seen him you love him; though you do not now see him you believe in him and rejoice with unutterable and exalted joy." [12]

CHAPTER NOTES:

1. John 20:19-23
2. John 20:24-25
3. Matt. 10:2
4. Mark 8:11-12
5. John 20:26-28
6. John 11:16
7. John 14:4-6
8. Told by William Barclay in *The Expository Times*
9. John 11:7-16
10. Published by the Student Christian Movement Press Ltd., London, 1953, p. 24
11. John 19:29
12. I Peter 1:8 R.S.V.

III

These Were Helped By Him

9
The Samaritan Woman

ON THE WEST bank of the River Jordan is a lump of land still known as Samaria; and you still have to pass through it, as Jesus did, when you travel between Galilee on the north and Judea on the south. The three hundred surviving Samaritans live there. They are Jews of mixed blood who have their own version of the Jewish religion, their own yearly Passover Feast on April 15th, their own synagogue and their own scroll of the Books of Moses which reputedly goes back to Moses himself, although it records his death.

The village of Sychar in Samaria became an Arab refugee camp after the establishment of the State of Israel in 1948. In the 1967 war the Israelis captured Samaria, and the refugees had to move out of Sychar and find a new refuge on the east bank of the Jordan.

The main building in Sychar is a walled enclosure that contains a church and a well that you reach by going down steps into a kind of cellar. This well, which is the only source of drinking water for miles around, was dug nearly four thousand years ago by the patriarch Jacob, and people have been quenching their thirst at it ever since. I quenched my thirst on a blistering hot day, then went up to the courtyard which is under the shadow of Mount Gerizim. I opened the New Testament at the fourth chapter of John's Gospel and read the story of Jesus and the Samaritan woman who came to that well to draw water. Suddenly I looked up and in my imagination saw her standing before me. I didn't confuse her with the Samaritan women whom I had met on the road, carrying pots on top of their heads and dressed in first-century clothing. This woman came right out of the Gospel story.[1]

She spoke first: "I can see that you are reading about me. Does my story interest you?"

"Interest me?" I replied, "I can recite it from memory."

That pleased her, and she said, "Do you want to know anything that isn't in the book?"

I was bursting with curiosity, so I said, "Yes, I want to know how you felt when you came to the well and saw Jesus sitting here, and he said, 'Give me a drink'."

She replied, "I was surprised. Surely you can guess that from the way I answered him, 'What! You, a Jew, ask a drink of me, a Samaritan woman?' As you know, we Samaritans were not friendly with Jews. Let's say the Jews were not friendly with us. They considered us racially impure and ritually unclean. They wouldn't eat from the same dishes. A religious Jew would die of thirst before drinking out of a cup that one of us had used. Yet this Jew said, 'Give me a drink.' A Jewish man, too. They didn't usually start a conversation with their own women, let alone one of ours, especially a woman like me. He had to know that something was wrong when I came to the well at noon by myself instead of in the evening with the other women. Yet he treated me as though I were a person, he asked me for a drink of water, he put himself in my debt, he accepted me."

"You were not accustomed to being accepted?"

"No, I was accustomed to being rejected — by everybody. I was a social outcast, like a leper. This man was so courteous that I thought he must be playing a game with me. I realised later that he was showing me that God accepts us just as we are. He doesn't ask us to become pious or religious or different. He doesn't ask us to go to a sacred building to meet him. He takes the initiative and comes to meet us right beside the well in the middle of the day. God is gracious as Jesus was gracious." She paused and said, "Are you still curious about me?"

I was very curious, so I asked her another question: "Jesus said to you, 'If only you knew what God gives, and who it is that is asking you for a drink, you would have asked him and

he would have given you living water'. And you replied, 'Sir,
you have no bucket, and the well is deep. How can you give
me "living water"? Are you a greater man than Jacob our
ancestor, who gave us the well, and drank from it himself...?'
Did you really mean that or were you being sarcastic?"

Almost as though she were a little ashamed of it the woman
replied, "I was being sarcastic, of course. I knew that he
wasn't talking about real water and I thought for a moment
that he wasn't interested in any kind of water. I suspected
that he was interested in me, as most men are when they
know how much I have been around, but his line was
different from the others. I thought, 'All right, brother, two
can play at that game,' and that's when I mentioned the
bucket. Then I decided that he was well-meaning but maybe
a do-gooder. He was not interested in my body but in my
soul. That was even worse. So I gave him a flippant answer."

"But you weren't being flippant when you said a moment
later, 'Sir, give me that water, and then I shall not be thirsty,
nor have to come all this way to draw.' It wasn't your way of
saying, 'I am tired of making this long journey to the well
every day. By all means put running water into my house, if
you can'."

"Oh no," she hastened to reply. "I really meant that. When
Jesus pointed to the well and said, 'Everyone who drinks this
water will be thirsty again, but whoever drinks the water that
I shall give him will never suffer thirst any more. The water
that I shall give him will be an inner spring always welling up
for eternal life' — when Jesus said that, I knew that he was
being serious and I became serious too. All of a sudden I
realised how thirsty I was. I had a thirst that no water, no
food, no money, no sex, nothing on this earth could ever
satisfy. I was thirsty for life, a cleaner, purer, better life than I
had ever known. I had wanted it for a long time and had
given up all hope, yet here was this stranger telling me about
a kind of water that could quench my thirst for life."

"Did you believe that Jesus could give you that living
water?"

"No, not at first, because I didn't know who he was. He
talked about eternal life. Only God gives eternal life, and God
and I weren't friends any more. We had fallen out a long time

ago. I didn't want anything to do with God and I was pretty
sure that he didn't want anything to do with me. What I
didn't realise was that I was seeing God in a new way. He not
only comes to meet you where you are, he not only accepts
you in spite of what you are, but he doesn't demand anything
at first, he makes an offer, a gracious offer. He makes you see
that the life you are living is not really life at all. He shows
you the kind of life that you really long for and awakens your
sense of need for it. That's what he did for me and that's why
I said, 'Sir, give me that water, and then I shall not be thirsty,
nor have to come all this way to draw'."

I hesitated to ask the next question, but her candid manner
seemed to encourage it. "Forgive me for being personal, but
were you embarrassed when Jesus said, 'Go home and call
your husband and come back'?"

She smiled and replied, "No, not at first. I thought that it
was something he wanted me to share with my family.
Religion is usually a man's affair in our society; and if he was
going to talk to me about religion, I supposed that he wanted
to talk it over with my husband. I simply said, 'I have no
husband.' Why tell him anything else? Let him think that I
was unmarried or a widow or once-divorced. What difference
could it make to him? Why burden him with all the sordid
details of my life?"

"Did it surprise you when Jesus knew them anyway?"

The woman hesitated, then said, "I couldn't have been
more surprised. I thought that nobody knew the whole story
of my life, not even the people in the village, let alone this
stranger who had never met me before. When he told me the
truth about myself, it was like hitting me a blow across the
face. It nearly knocked me down. He said, 'You are right in
saying that you have no husband, for although you have had
five husbands, the man with whom you are now living is not
your husband; you told me the truth there'. There was a long
silence after that. I wanted the ground to swallow me up. He
wasn't being insulting or judgmental like most religious
teachers of our time. He was more like a doctor diagnosing a
disease and saying, 'Here is your trouble. We must deal with
it if you want to be made well.' I didn't try to explain it to
him."

"Would you care to explain it to me?"

She brightened for a moment and said, "Yes, I would. I don't want you to think that I was a polygamist or even a loose woman. I was married to five husbands, one after the other, but it's not as bad as it sounds. The first was a very old man. My father owed him a lot of money and gave me to him as a payment. He died, then I married a soldier, and he was killed in the very next battle. I can explain the others too. As for the common-law relationship in which I was living when I met Jesus — I knew that was wrong but I didn't want to give it up. It was my only security. Even a woman like me has to live."

"Did Jesus tell you to give it up?" I asked.

"No", she replied, "it wasn't that way at all. He didn't tell me that I had to do anything. He didn't need to. I saw him and I saw myself and I felt unclean in his presence. He had exposed my great problem, forced me to face the truth; and I knew that I would have to deal with it if I wanted the kind of life that he was offering me. But I didn't have the courage to deal with it — not then. Some changes are just too great to make, and who knows if they are going to be worthwhile?"

"So you tried to change the subject instead?"

"I had to," she said honestly. "The conversation was becoming too personal and too uncomfortable. Jesus knew all about me. I guessed that he was a religious teacher, and it seemed a good idea to get him talking about religion. That's always a safe subject. I pointed to the mountain and said to him, 'Sir, I can see that you are a prophet. Our fathers worshipped on this mountain, but you Jews say that the temple where God should be worshipped is in Jerusalem'. I thought that if I could just get him into a discussion about the correct place to worship God, it might take attention off me and my problems. Surely you have tried that ploy."

Now the Samaritan woman had put me on the spot, and I had to be honest with her. I said, "Yes, it's a strange thing about religion. It's supposed to bring us to God and yet it very often stands between us and God. People still get interested in religion as a means of avoiding the problems of their own lives. They get terribly excited about hymn tunes and terribly apathetic about human suffering. They spend hours solving the problems of the Church and no time at all solving the problems of their families. They never seem to realise that God is more interested in them than in creeds and liturgies and forms of church administration."

"Yes," she replied, "that's what Jesus told me. He said, in effect, 'If you want to talk about worship, we shall do so, but remember this: God is spirit, and those who worship him must worship in spirit and in truth.' He was saying that the place and techniques of worship do not matter. What does matter is the sincerity of your worship, the reality of your communion with God. More than all your words and prayers and praises God wants your life, and you had better ask yourself whether the life you are now living is acceptable to him. My ploy of changing the subject didn't work, because there is only one subject in religion. *That subject is you*, and you can't change it."

"So then you tried another ploy."

"Yes, I tried the old trick of postponing the issue. Some day I would have to face God, but not right now. You know the prayer, 'God, make me pure, but not yet.' I assumed that as a Jewish prophet Jesus would be mainly interested, as all devout Jews were, in the coming of the Messiah, so I became pious and said, 'I know that the Messiah is coming. When he comes he will tell us everything.' That would be time enough to put my life in order, and that time might never come. I could postpone dealing with my personal problems until then. After all, I wasn't being different from any person who wants to enjoy life for a while before taking inventory of his soul. Some day he will make peace with God but right now he is too busy making money and making pleasure. Yes, I wanted the better life that Jesus offered and I knew that I would have to pay a price for it but I would wait for the moment of truth. What I didn't realise was that my moment of truth had come there and then."

My conversation with this woman of Samaria had also reached its moment of truth. I said to her, "When you told Jesus that you were waiting for the Messiah, and he replied, 'I am he, I who am speaking to you now,' did you realise that apart from John the Baptist you were the first person in history to whom Jesus disclosed himself as the long-awaited

Messiah of Israel foretold in the Scriptures? Up to this point even his disciples had not recognised him. Many people have never recognised him."

"I came to realise it later," she said, "and I still can't understand why he should have chosen me of all people on earth to be the first to know the truth about him. But I have to confess that in that moment I wasn't thinking about Israel or history or the Scriptures. I was thinking about myself and I believe that Jesus was thinking about me too. He was different from all that I had been brought up to believe about the Messiah. He wasn't an angel or a political leader, he was a person who brought God into my experience and offered me the gift of eternal life and showed me what I must do to accept it. And I knew that I had to accept it then or not at all. There could be no postponing the issue. Jesus had come into my life and he might never come again. This was my chance, perhaps my only chance. We don't choose the time and place of our conversion, God chooses it."

As the Samaritan woman finished speaking, I glanced again at the story in John's Gospel and said, "It doesn't say anything here about your conversion. What do you mean by it? How were you converted?"

She replied, "I turned around, that's all. I changed the direction of my life. It wasn't an emotional experience. My spirit had been drained of emotions long ago. No tears, just a conscious decision to accept the life that Jesus offered and pay the price to receive it."

Still looking at the New Testament, I said, "The story says that you went back to the village and said to the people, 'Come and see a man who told me everything I ever did. Could this be the Messiah?' Surely it wasn't easy for you to do that?"

"It was the most difficult thing I have done," she replied. "I wasn't on speaking terms with the respectable people in the village. They wouldn't be seen talking to me. Yet the amazing thing is that they listened to what I had to say. They didn't argue, didn't doubt, they just came to the well and met Jesus as I had met him and were captured by him as I was captured. He stayed for two days in our village, and I faded into the back of the picture. Some of the people were kind enough to say to me, 'It is no longer because of what you said that we believe, for we have heard him ourselves, and we know that this is in truth the Saviour of the world'."

"So, your fellow-citizens, even though they didn't respect you very much, had cause to be grateful that you introduced them to Jesus."

"They said so," she replied, "but I think that I did it more for my sake than for theirs. If I wanted them to accept me and believe that I was really changed, I had to introduce them to the person who changed me. I knew that it was going to be difficult starting life all over again. I might fail sometimes, and when people saw my failures they would shake their heads doubtfully and say, 'You see, she hasn't really changed at all.' But they wouldn't doubt for long because they wouldn't think about me. They would think about Jesus. My life would be a window through which people would look and see Jesus. I guess that's what it means to witness to him."

CHAPTER NOTES:
1.   John 4:1-42

10
The Canaanite Woman

What is a Great Faith?

HAVE YOU EVER known of a person whose character could be summed up in four words? You have never met that person; he lived and died long before you were born; but if those four words were inscribed as an epitaph on his tombstone they would tell you everything you need to know about him. It depends, of course, upon whether the words were spoken by a friend or an enemy, a critic or an admirer. Some people are more qualified than others to pronounce judgment. If a newspaper critic says after the death of a concert pianist, "He was a failure," you murmur to yourself, "Well, that's one man's opinion." If a great musician says, "He was a genius," you take that remark seriously.

There is a character in the Gospel drama to whom Jesus said four memorable words — *"Great is your faith."*[1] She was a Canaanite woman who came from the country north of Palestine, a country hostile to the Jews; she was presumably married, she had at least one child, but that's all we know about her. We don't know whether she was a good woman or a bad woman. We don't know her name. We only know that in her single encounter with Jesus he said to her, "Great is your faith."

Only four words, but they were enough to make her immortal. For nineteen centuries people have stood beside the grave of this nameless woman and read the words which history has inscribed on her tombstone — "She had a great faith." That's all, but they tell us everything we need to know about her, and we can trust them because Jesus spoke them. He was an expert on faith. He searched for faith as a gem-collector searches for fine jewels and, when he found it, he was filled with joy. He did not always find it in his disciples. On no occasion did he say to Peter, John or James, "Great is your faith." Rather he said, in effect, "If only you had a little faith like a grain of mustard seed..."[2] Only in one other character, also a non-Jew, a Roman officer stationed in Capernaum, did Jesus find a faith worthy of unlimited praise.[3] Only to a nameless woman from the region of Tyre and Sidon did he actually say, "Great is your faith," or as the New English Bible puts it, "Woman, what faith you have!"

We regard her with more than an academic interest. She awakens within us a feeling of admiration, perhaps of envy, because she stands where many of us would like to stand. A great faith is precisely what we do not have. We know that faith can move mountains but we know also that we don't have enough faith to move molehills. Going back to the musical metaphor, think what it would mean to an aspiring young artist if one of the world's leading musicians put his hand on his shoulder and said to him, "You have a great gift." Think what it would mean to a believer in God if he heard the voice of Christ saying to him, "You have a great faith." But how does one qualify for that word of praise? By what remarkable process does one reach the condition of mind and heart that can be described as a great faith? What does one have to do? What did the Canaanite woman do? In what did her faith consist?

Crossing a Barrier

Her faith consisted mainly in the fact that she turned to Jesus for help. That was remarkable when you remember that she was a Gentile, a Canaanite, and therefore a traditional enemy of the Jews. It was an emnity as real and deep-seated as that existing between the modern Israeli Jews and their Arab neighbours. You may wonder what Jesus was doing in her country; on no other occasion did he step outside Jewish territory. The common explanation is that he knew that he was coming to the end of his earthly ministry and he needed privacy to train the disciples to carry it on after his death. He couldn't find that privacy in Palestine, so he went into Gentile territory where people didn't know him or else would pay no attention to him because he was a Jew. Canaanites

were no more likely to consult him as a physician than a
Palestinian Arab is likely to put his life in the hands of an
Israeli doctor today. The prejudices went too deep and the
barriers rose too high. Yet here was a woman who in her
desperate need was prepared to cross a barrier and turn to Jesus
for help. That was her faith.

Faith still consists in turning to Jesus for help and it still consists
in crossing a barrier, several barriers, to reach him. There is the
barrier of time, two thousand years to be precise, which is a wide
gulf to cross without the aid of a time-machine. Jesus lived then,
we live now, and life has become a different ball-game. How can
he possibly help us? There is the barrier of culture. A generation
that travels faster than the speed of sound may wonder how it can
get help for its problems from a Palestinian peasant who rode into
Jerusalem on the back of a borrowed donkey. Does he even
understand our problems? There is the barrier of pride. In a world
where we have gained more and more mastery over nature we feel
less and less inclined to look for help in supernature. We feel like
the old man who said to a well-meaning woman, when she
suggested that he turn to Jesus for help, "I don't need no help
from Jesus. I'm doing all right by myself."

The Canaanite woman knew that she wasn't doing all right
by herself, and that's why she was willing to cross a barrier to
Jesus. She cried out to him, "Sir! have pity on me, Son of
David; my daughter is tormented by a devil." Her predicament
becomes very real in the light of *The Exorcist*,[4] the best-selling
paperback novel that was made into a motion picture which so
far has netted a hundred million dollars. It is the story of a
sophisticated woman in Washington, an actress separated from
her husband, whose twelve-year-old daughter, normally a quiet
and cheerful child, began showing strange symptoms of behaviour. Out of her mouth came the most revolting obscenities
and blasphemies. Her features contorted, and she spoke with
the croaking voice of an old man. She became so violent and
physically ill that they had to strap her to the bed which moved
up and down of its own accord. Physicians and psychiatrists
were baffled by her behaviour, and her mother nearly went out
of her mind. Finally, at her wits' end, she consulted a priest who
concluded against all reason that the child was possessed by a
devil which must be exorcised. The woman was not

a believer, she didn't understand demon-possession and the Church's ritual of exorcism, but she was desperate, and her desperation drove her to Christ's representative for help.

Neither did the Canaanite woman understand Jesus when she turned to him for help. At first she addressed him by a human title, 'Sir", then by a popular title, "Son of David". She had heard that he was a good and powerful man who had done wonderful things for other people, so she put aside her prejudice and pride and turned to him because she was desperate, she had no other hope. That was her faith and it was enough. That is still the essence of faith. There is no great exercise of the intellect involved in it. You don't have to recite the Apostles' Creed or accept the Doctrine of the Trinity or believe in miracles or even feel an emotion of trust in your heart. You simply come to Christ in a situation where you have exhausted all human resources and stretch out your hands to him, saying, "Have pity on me."

Refusing to be Put Off

We can go a step further and say that the woman's faith consisted in her refusal to be intimidated. There were at least three intimidating factors. One of them was the silence of Jesus. The story tells us that to her outstretched hand, her humble appeal, her desperate sense of need, her plea for pity, Jesus "said not a word in reply". He snubbed her. How unlike him! That in itself should have been enough to turn her away. There is no reaction harder to bear than silence, simply because it is not a reaction but a rebuff. A flat "No" you can take, because at least it acknowledges your presence and tells you where you stand; but when you go to someone for help and he keeps silent, you don't know what he is thinking or if he heard you or even noticed that you are there. That can be devastating.

There is no sterner test of faith than the silence of God; and that silence can be very real in the experience of a true believer, especially a person who prays. It was very real to Job of the Old Testament, sitting on his ash heap outside the village and scraping scabs off his leprous body. He could have stood his suffering if only the Almighty had not gone into hiding and shut off all communication. Again and again he shook his fist against heaven and challenged God to come out and answer him.[5] Pleading with God can be like talking in a telephone and suddenly suspecting that the party at the other end of the line is not there any more. He hasn't bothered to hang up the receiver, he has just gone away or turned his attention to more important matters because he is not interested in what you have to say.

That's how it was with the Canaanite woman. She told Jesus that her daughter was crazy, and Jesus "said not a word in reply". No dial tone, just silence. But her faith consisted in the fact that she refused to be intimidated by that silence; instead, she reached behind it and spoke to the great heart of God. She perceived what very few people have the faith to perceive — that the silence of God does not denote his indifference. Even in our human relationships silence can be an eloquent response, a sure sign of sympathy and understanding. As long as Job's friends kept silent they comforted him; it was when they began to talk that they rubbed salt into his wounds. That's why he said to them, "Ah, if only you would be silent, and let silence be your wisdom."[6] We are not to lose faith when God says nothing to us in our suffering; it may be the surest sign that God is suffering with us.

Another intimidating factor for the Canaanite woman was that she received no help from the disciples. On the contrary, they couldn't take her misery, they regarded her as a nuisance and they urged Jesus, "Send her away; see how she comes shouting after us." They said the same thing when they saw the five thousand hungry people on the shore of the Sea of Galilee. "Send the people off to the farms and villages round about to buy themselves something to eat."[7] That has often been the Church's reaction to human suffering, to the homeless, the hungry, the helpless people of society who stretch out their hands and plead for pity. "Send them away to the prisons, the ghettos, the hospitals, the theatres, the gaming casinos, the welfare agencies — anywhere as long as they get out of our sight and stop shouting after us." The Church develops compassion fatigue, it becomes weary of the continual presentation of human suffering — which is one reason why many people today call the Church irrelevant, one reason why they have rejected the Church and rejected God. But the Canaanite woman was not going to be put off by the Church's indifference. She wasn't dealing with the Church but with the Church's Lord. That was her faith.

Yet it was the Church's Lord who seemed most intimidating to her. He behaved like a Pharisee, not like the friend of publicans and sinners. When he finally broke the silence and spoke to the woman he said something that has to be seen in print to be believed: "I was sent to the lost sheep of the house of Israel, and to them alone." On a pilgrimage to the Holy Land a member of our party suffered a heart attack. We took her to a hospital in Jerusalem where an Israeli doctor treated her with skill and concern. Suppose he had turned her away, saying, in effect, "I was sent to the lost sheep of the house of Israel, and to them alone." That would have been not only bigoted but heartless. Was Jesus testing the woman or trying to bring her to the true faith, as some commentators suggest? Whatever the Master's motive, it must have sounded to her as though he were saying, "Sorry madam, but you are not a religious woman. You don't belong. You have no claim on me."

That can be intimidating even when you say it to yourself. In one of my parishes I used to take Communion regularly to a lady who had been a bed-ridden cripple for many years. Her husband took care of her with the most loving devotion. He always sat beside his wife during our private Communion Services. Whenever I asked if he also would receive the Sacrament, he always replied, "No. I am not a religious man. I don't belong to the Church". How terribly tragic if people could actually cut themselves off from the grace of God by saying, "We don't belong"! How infinitely more tragic if they thought that Jesus was saying it to them, as he said it to the Canaanite woman! Her faith consisted in the fact that Jesus did say it and she refused to be put off by it. Though not a religious woman and therefore unable to speak the right words, she could let her need speak for itself. In spite of what Jesus said about the lost sheep of Israel, she fell at his feet and cried, "Help me, sir." That was her faith and it is the essence of all faith — to stretch out your hand to God's Christ, whether or not you belong to the Church and believe the right dogmas, and let your need plead with him for pity.

Making No Claim

We can take one more step and discover a still deeper

ingredient in this woman's remarkable faith. It comes out in her response to the next statement of Jesus, and again we have difficulty believing that he actually said it. To her cry, "Help me, sir," he replied, "It is not right to take the children's bread and throw it to the dogs." That sounds like a contemptuous insult in any man's language. Even today we reserve the term "dog" or one of its synonyms for someone whom we particularly despise. It has been pointed out that Jesus used the diminutive word meaning household pets which were very different from the wild animals that roamed the streets and probed the garbage heaps. It has been pointed out also that he probably spoke with compassion in his voice and a smile on his face, that he didn't really mean to insult her but was teasing her in order to test her faith. Some test! It must have sounded to the poor woman as though he were saying even more emphatically, "Sorry, madam. You don't qualify. You have no claim on the good things that God has given me for his children." We could understand it if at that point the woman had burst into tears and walked away.

But she didn't cry and she didn't walk away. Instead, she gave Jesus an answer that must have excited him like an electric charge going through his whole body. "True, sir", she answered. She didn't stop there, but we are going to stop there for a moment as we would stop to admire a fine jewel, because there is no more shining example of what the Bible means by faith. One thing you can say about such faith — it's at the opposite end of the pole from pride. If Jesus or anyone else answered *my* plea for help by saying, "It is not right to take the children's bread and throw it to the dogs," I might burst into tears, I might fly into a rage, I might walk away in a huff; but the last thing I should do is swallow my pride and say to him, "True, sir, I admit that I am a dog." The Canaanite woman was not admitting to being a dog — she knew that Jesus wasn't really calling her a dog — but she was saying, in effect, "True, sir, I admit that I have no claim on you." That was her faith and it is still faith — to go to God and ask for his help, letting your need speak for you, but admitting that you have no claim on him. God may help you but he doesn't have to help. You can make no demands.

Then the woman added a matchless reply that must have

delighted the heart of Jesus. "True, sir, and yet the dogs eat the scraps that fall from their masters' table." If Jesus wasn't smiling up to that point, he certainly smiled then. Talk about repartee! The woman was a genius. Even in her distraught state of mind she could return exactly the right answer, she could respond to the Master's humour with a humour all of her own, she could display a sparkling sense of wit. "It is not right to take the children's bread and throw it to the dogs." "True, sir, and yet the dogs eat the scraps that fall from their masters' table." How could Jesus resist that charming and winsome appeal? Wasn't she saying, "Yes, I admit that I have no claim on your regular bounty, but there must be some extra, some grace that I don't deserve, and I am appealing to you for that"? No wonder Jesus replied, "Woman, what faith you have! Be it as you wish!" No wonder that from that moment her daughter was restored to health.

Other translations of the Bible Story (e.g. K.J.V. and R.S.V.) have the woman addressing Jesus as "Lord", which indicates a remarkable evolution of faith in her brief encounter. The greatness of her faith consisted in many factors, not least of all her insight into Jesus himself, her recognition, of the person to whom she was speaking. Whatever the form of address, she treated him as her Lord. She knew that he could turn a deaf ear to her plea for pity, that he could refuse to heal her demented daughter, *but would he*, being what he was and what he claimed to be? A two-way test took place in that encounter. Jesus tested her faith; she tested the promises of God. She took the Saviour at his word. Martin Luther says that "she threw the sack of his promises down at his feet". To go to God and say to him, "I need your help and I ask for it, not because of what I am but because of the promises you have made in Jesus Christ our Lord" — *that* is a great faith.

CHAPTER NOTES:

1. Matt. 15:21-28, v.28 (R.S.V.)   5. Job 31:35
2. Matt. 17:20   6. Job 13:5
3. Matt. 8:10   7. Mark 6:35
4. William Peter Blatty
    The Exorcist, (Harper & Row Inc,
    New York, 1971)

11
The Man Born Blind

What is a Great Witness?

WHAT DO THESE people have in common? The first is a business man who speaks for five minutes on a weekly television programme sponsored by the Chicago Sunday Evening Club. He owns and operates a large janitorial firm that specialises in cleaning hospitals and he tells the audience about the main business of his life which is to serve Jesus Christ. The second is a university student discussing religion in the small hours of the morning with some other students. He says, "I don't know about you fellows, but my life had no real purpose until I found Jesus Christ." The third is a nineteen-year-old Russian girl who stands on the main street of Leningrad on a bitterly cold winter day handing out cards printed with religious poetry which she has written. What do those people have in common?

The answer is that they are witnessing to their religious faith. The word "witness" is one of those honoured words in the Christian vocabulary which has lost currency in the main-line Churches perhaps because it has lost its original meaning. In legal terminology a witness is someone who saw an event and was therefore part of the event and who stands up in court and says, "This is how it happened." Jesus gave it the same meaning when he said, in effect, to his disciples, "You have seen the event of my life, death and resurrection. You have seen it happen, you are a part of it, you are characters in the redemption drama. Therefore you must tell other people the truth about it. You shall be my witnesses." [1]

Christ calls every Christian to witness in that true sense;

and a committed Christian wants to know not only how to witness but how to make a great witness. Let him look, then, at a nameless character in the Gospel drama who was truly a supporting character of Jesus and whose single appearance on the stage is described in the ninth chapter of John.[2] This man demonstrates what it means to witness to Jesus Christ. As the Canaanite woman showed us a great faith,[3] here is a man who shows us a great witness.

He was one of the people whom Jesus helped during his earthly ministry, one of the blind men to whom the Great Physician gave the gift of sight. Jesus was always healing blind men, probably because in his day more people suffered from blindness than from any other affliction. Even now the blind man is a familiar figure in the land of our Lord's birth. Little wonder that the prophets of Israel foretold that one of the great blessings to be brought by God's Messiah would be "recovery of sight for the blind",[4] and that Jesus himself, pointing to the signs of his Messiahship, sent word to John the Baptist, saying, "Tell John that the blind recover their sight."[5] Of all the blind men whom Jesus healed, only the man in John's Gospel emerged as a distinct personality. We know something about his case history, we know that he participated in his cure. We know also that there was an aftermath to his cure, a little drama in which he played the leading role and in which he showed us what it means to be a great witness.

A Story To Tell

A great witness is a person with a story to tell. He declares what God has done for him. He is not the disputatious type who has read a few books and goes around picking arguments with people and trying to persuade them that he has all the answers. He doesn't pretend to know *all* the answers — only the answers for himself. He doesn't foist his opinions on everybody else. In a quiet, convincing way he simply tells what has happened to him in his encounter with Jesus Christ. He speaks out of a first-hand experience.

The former blind man spoke out of a tremendous experience. He was not only blind but he had never been anything else. He was born blind and was stigmatised for his affliction.

We sympathise with such a person, but the Jews of Jesus' day believed that a man blind from his birth must have sinned in his mother's womb or inherited the sins of his fathers. Even the disciples asked Jesus, "Rabbi, who sinned, this man or his parents?" Blind people today, by developing their remaining senses, can lead full, rich, useful and happy lives; but in Jesus' day a blind man could not perform even the most menial role. He was condemned to beg. There was no such thing as surgery or medical treatment that gave him the hope of ever being able to see. Only a miracle could rescue him from perpetual darkness, and that's what happened to him when he met Jesus. That was his first-hand experience.

It was a dramatic miracle even in its technique. Jesus didn't simply wave his hand in front of the man's face and say, "You can see". He spat on the ground and made a muddy ointment which he pasted on the sightless eyes. That may sound unhygienic until we remember that in the ancient world it was believed that the spittle of a distinguished person possessed curative qualities. Then he told the blind man to wash in the Pool of Siloam, a small body of water outside the present wall of Jerusalem which Arab urchins still use as a swimming bath. The man did what he was told, and suddenly God switched on the lights. For the first time a whole world became visible to the man's eyes. All his life he had recognised people by their voices. Now for the first time he saw what a human face and hand looked like. All his life he had recognised flowers by their smell. Now for the first time he looked on the beauty of a flower. He had been told that the sky is blue. Now he looked upward and said, "So that's what blue is." It was like being born a second time. He must have been delirious with joy.

That's the story that he had to tell. He didn't go around preaching sermons or performing acts of mercy to convince people that he was a follower of Jesus. He didn't know anything about Jesus. He didn't know who Jesus was and he didn't care. That's what he told the Pharisees when they tried to make him confess that Jesus was a sinner: "Whether or not he is a sinner, I do not know. All I know is this: once I was blind, now I can see." You hear that refrain all through the New Testament. "Once I was a tax-collector, now I am an honest man.".[6] "Once I was a cripple, now I can walk".[7] "Once I was a whore, now I am a pure woman".[8] It is the first-hand testimony of something wonderful which has happened to a person because Jesus Christ has entered his experience; and it is a great witness because no one can argue against it.

D.R. Davies had a story to tell. He was a Church of England clergyman who wrote his autobiography under the title, *In Search of Myself.* He began his career as a Congregational minister but he was not a very convincing minister because he wasn't very convinced. After emptying a couple of churches he drifted into journalism and politics. He became a humanist, a socialist, a Marxist, an atheist. He fought in the Spanish Civil War, saw the break-up of his marriage and even tried to commit suicide. He found his way back but not along the old roads of intellectual discovery. This time he came to Christ along the new path of personal experience, and his ministry became a great witness. He writes,

> Now I had a first-hand experience of the power of Christ, a
> first-hand knowledge of God. For that experience I had to
> pay a great price in terms of human frustration, defeat and
> suffering. But the pearl was mine. Now I had a faith that
> could stand up to any disaster time could bring. I was able
> to do the one essential of the ministerial calling, namely, to
> witness to the redeeming power of Jesus Christ. Now I felt I
> could take my place on the witness-stand and say: 'Yes!
> This is true: Christ can and does save men from despair
> and gloom. He has done it to me'. Amid all the complexity
> and confusion of our time, I am forever sure of the
> redeeming power of God in Christ. Though all the world
> were to unite in denying this, I should still be certain. This
> one thing I know, whereas I was blind, now I see...[9]

Standing Alone

The man born blind shows us also that the great witness is the person who stands most alone. He certainly stood alone. People not only failed to support him, they turned against him. His neighbours could not even identify him as the man who used to sit and beg, which indicates that they hadn't even noticed his existence as a human being. The religious leaders openly resented his cure. His parents, for fear of the religious leaders, refused to become involved. "He is of age," they said, "he will speak for himself." Was there nobody to come forward and exclaim, "My dear man, you can see. How wonderful. Let's celebrate"? No! Stern glares all around him, as though to say, "What do you mean by crawling out of your cave of blindness? How dare you allow Jesus to open your eyes?"

That seems heartless enough. Then you look ahead a few months and see the same people, or others like them, nailing Jesus to a cross. If ever a man stood alone with every man's hand against him, it was Jesus during the last twelve hours of his earthly life — condemned by the priests, betrayed by a disciple, denied by another disciple, deserted by his friends, jeered at by the crowds and sentenced to death in place of a murderer. In varying degrees that has often been the fate of a good man empowered by God to witness for God before his fellow-men. Instead of rejoicing with him they resent and ostracise him. He is the man who stands most alone.

Leslie Weatherhead tells of meeting a young Indian army chaplain during the First World War. The chaplain said that when he decided to become a Christian, his whole village blazed up in anger. To make him recant, they tied him to a pillar in the courtyard of his parents' house, stripped the turban from his head, which is a mark of indignity in the East, lashed his back with whips until the blood ran, and left him standing hour after hour under the burning sun. They even had the contents of a sewage bin poured over his head. When the men had done their worst, he was subjected to another kind of torture. His aged mother came out and pleaded with him. "My son," she cried. "I bore you, I brought you up, I love you. You can't bring such pain and shame to me at the end of my life." The young man tenderly told her that he had found One who loved him even more than she did and that he felt he must remain loyal to Christ. For years, even after he became a distinguished minister of the Church in India, he remained an outcast from his own people. When he tried to visit his relatives, they would not

receive him. Like the man born blind, who accepted the gift
of sight from the hand of Jesus, he stood alone. That was his
witness.[10]

There is something very powerful in that lonely witness.
The playwright Ibsen makes one of his characters say, "I will
go so far as to say that I am the strongest man in the whole
world... You see, I have made a great discovery... It is this.
Let me tell you. That the strongest man in the world is he
that stands most alone."[11] Perhaps that is why Archbishop
Helder Camera is one of the strongest men in Brazil today.
He stands most alone. Jesus stood most alone on Good
Friday, and because of his loneliness he was the strongest man
in the world, the strongest man in history. There is power in
moral loneliness, in being a person whom other people resent
because you have found Christ and are therefore not like the
rest of them. It is not always a happy state but it's a great
witness.

Speaking with Courage

The man born blind shows that the great witness is the
person who speaks up with courage. Because it was the
Sabbath Day, the Pharisees, the policemen of the Sabbath,
assembled in a court of inquiry and summoned the man to
appear before them. They wanted to know exactly how the
alleged miracle of healing took place. When he told them
about Jesus spreading paste on his eyes and instructing him
to wash in the pool, the coin dropped in their bigoted minds.
Here was clearly a case of Sabbath-breaking. The healer was
a sinner, so how could he have performed the miracle? "What
have you to say about him?" they asked. "It was your eyes he
opened." The man answered, "He is a prophet", meaning a
man of God.

Certain that the man must be lying, they summoned his
parents. "Is this man your son? Do you say that he was born
blind? How is it that he can see now?" You would expect
them to reply, "Yes, he is our son. He was born blind, and we
have felt guilty and heartbroken over it. He can see now
because Jesus opened his eyes. Praise be to Jesus!" Instead,
they virtually dissociated themselves from their son and his

healer. "Ask him; he is of age; he will speak for himself."
Obviously they feared the Pharisees, and with good reason,
"for the Jewish authorities had already agreed that anyone
who acknowledged Jesus as Messiah should be banned from
the synagogue."

The Pharisees turned again to the blind beggar. Though
not questioning the miraculous cure itself, they demanded
that he give praise only to God and admit Jesus to be a
sinner. That's like telling a patient, cured of glaucoma today,
to call his eye surgeon a man of loose moral character. He
doesn't care about his healer's character. "Whether or not he
is a sinner, I do not know. All I know is this: once I was blind,
now I can see." That angered the religious bloodhounds who
again demanded that he describe in detail exactly how Jesus
was supposed to have cured him. Impatiently and boldly he
retorted, "I have told you already, but you took no notice.
Why do you want to hear it again? Do you also want to
become his disciples?" That sent their Pharisaic blood-
pressure soaring. "We are disciples of Moses," they exploded.
"We know that God spoke to Moses, but as for this fellow, we
do not know where he comes from."

"All right, Mr. Man-Born-Blind, shut up now and give
them the last word. That will satisfy them." But how do you
shut up a man in the delirium of new birth? How do you
persuade him to renounce his benefactor? The former beggar's boldness now carried him to a point of sarcasm. "What
an extraordinary thing!" he exclaimed. "Here is a man who
has opened my eyes. Yet you do not know where he comes
from... To open the eyes of a blind man — it is unheard of
since time began. If that man had not come from God he
could do nothing." Down came the big stick. "Who are you
to give us lessons," they retorted, "born and bred in sin as you
are?" Then they expelled him from the synagogue.

"There you are, Mr. Man-Born-Blind! We told you not to
open your big mouth." Yet we can't help admiring the
courage of his witness. He didn't belong to the silent majority
who say, "We don't talk about our religion any more. We let
our lives speak. We don't evangelise. We witness through
caring." Christ had done something for this man, released
him from darkness and ushered him into a world of light and

given his life meaning and usefulness, and he wanted everyone to hear about it. A great witness doesn't shut up, he speaks up. A Methodist pastor in India wrote a letter to an American magazine expressing his amazement over the new reticence of Christians today to speak up for Jesus Christ, epecially in former missionary lands. He said, "Somehow I have not yet understood that I am being self-righteous when I tell another person of what I could not do for myself at all, but what God in Jesus Christ has done for me. If I tell a sick man that I once had the same disease, but I found a doctor who wonderfully healed me, am I being self-righteous when I add that I think the same doctor can heal him?"[12]

Those three people whom we met at the beginning are not fictitious. The Russian girl is Aida Skrypnikova. When last heard of, she was in a prison camp three hundred miles east of Moscow. That was her second imprisonment. Both times the authorities arrested her for refusing to keep her mouth shut. She is a Christian, a rare breed in Russia, and she persists in telling everyone about it. To a leading newspaper she wrote, "As regards your anti-religious propaganda, we Christians do not fear it nor oppose it. Do you think a person who has really accepted Christ in his heart will be deceived by your lies?" The paper called her a religious fanatic and probably had something to do with her being imprisoned. For starting a prayer and Bible study group in the prison she was given ten days in solitary confinement. One of her fellow-prisoners said, "She speaks to everyone about Jesus." That is a great witness.[13]

Commitment to Christ

The man born blind shows us that the great witness is the person who commits himself in faith to Jesus Christ. He had no other alternative, no one he could trust. He had been expelled from the synagogue; and that was the severest penalty that could be inflicted on a first-century Jew, a far worse fate than physical blindness. A blind man was at least an accepted member of society. People pitied and helped him; but now that he had been excommunicated, no one would befriend him or do business with him or give him work or associate with him in any way. More seriously still, he would be cut off from his religious heritage and forbidden to worship the God of his fathers in the believing community. For the rest of his days he must live in ignoble isolation, deprived of status and liberty and privilege. Left in this predicament, his second state would be worse than his first.

Here Jesus re-entered the drama. Hearing of the man's courage and loneliness and subsequent punishment, Jesus came looking for him; and that in itself is significant. Jesus never leaves any man to bear his witness alone. He seeks him out and supports him and continually confirms him in his faith. Indeed, if a man's witness separates him from his fellow-men it brings him closer to Christ than ever he was before. " 'Have you faith in the Son of Man?' he asked. The man answered, 'Tell me who he is, sir, that I should put my faith in him.' 'You have seen him,' said Jesus, 'indeed, it is he who is speaking to you.' 'Lord, I believe,' he said and bowed before him."

Then Jesus administered a second cure. Having restored his physical vision, the Great Physician now opened the eyes of his soul. To the man born blind he not only revealed the truth about himself but made what have become to us the most precious promises of the Gospel, promises that make it possible for us to go on witnessing. "*I am the door*",[14] said Jesus. If ever the door of orthodox religion is slammed in our faces, let us have faith in Christ and we shall see that he is the entrance to the truth about God. "*I am the good shepherd*,"[15] said Jesus. If ever the people around us withhold their protecting care, let us have faith in Christ and we shall see that he is the true shepherd of our souls. "*I am the light of the world*,"[16] said Jesus. If ever the world envelops us in the darkness of resentment and hostility, let us have faith in Christ, and in his friendship we shall find the light of life. To trust those promises and live on the basis of them — that's what it means to be a great witness.

Bruce Marsh was a well-known Canadian broadcaster who died in 1974. For years he had suffered from a defective heart and he knew that he might not live beyond middle-age. Doctors raised his hopes by recommending him for a transplant. In fact, he spent the last months of his life at the

Stanford Medical Centre in California, waiting for the gift of a new heart. He died before it became available. In his interviews on radio, television and in the newspapers he spoke frankly of the resources which enabled him and his family to face the probability of his untimely death. Always he said, "We are Christians. We believe in Jesus Christ. We believe that Christ rose from the dead. We believe in the life everlasting." That affected people profoundly, even people who were worldly and sophisticated and made no profession of religious faith. In a spiritual sense it gave new heart to countless Christians. Bruce Marsh had committed himself in faith to Jesus Christ. That was his great witness.

CHAPTER NOTES:

1. Acts 1:8 (R.S.V.)
2. John 9:1-41
3. Matt. 15:21-28
4. Luke 4:18
5. Matt. 11:4
6. Luke 19:1-10
7. Mark 2:1-12
8. Luke 7:36-50
9. D.R. Davies,
   In Search of Myself
   (Geoffrey Bles, London, 1961) p. 200
10. Leslie D. Weatherhead,
    Personalities of the Passion
    (Hodder and Stoughton Ltd., London, 1942) pp. 84-86
11. Henrik Ibsen,
    An Enemy of the People
12. David B. Bauman in
    The Christian Century,
    May 31, 1972,
    pp. 638-639
13. "The Modern Martyr of Leningrad" by Leonard E. Le Sourd, Printed in *Guideposts* July, 1970, pp. 18-20
14. John 10:7
15. John 10:11
16. John 9:5

12
The Woman at Bethany

THERE IS NO doubt that the incident actually happened in some location and at some time during Jesus' ministry. All four Gospel writers record it with few variations.[1] A woman, whom John identifies as Mary the Sister of Martha and Lazarus, and whom some traditions identify as Mary Magdalene, anointed Jesus with costly ointment, much to the disgust of the spectators who deplored her extravagance, saying that the ointment might better have been sold and the proceeds given to the poor. The first three Gospels locate the incident at the house of Simon, a Pharisee, who presumably had a cancerous spot on his cheek and was known as Simon the Leper. Three writers date it during the last week of Jesus' earthly life and, though they recognise no motive for the woman's devotion, they have Jesus accepting it as the anointing of his body prior to its burial. They also suggest that it triggered off Judas' final betrayal. Luke dates the incident earlier in Jesus' ministry and, though he does not identify the woman, he does clearly designate her as "a woman who was living an immoral life in the town" and he interprets her act as a gesture of loving gratitude to Jesus who forgave her sins.

As in the case of the Samaritan woman, we know nothing about the nameless and fascinating woman of Bethany apart from her single appearance in the Gospel drama. Again we can only use our imagination to fill in the details. Conversing with her across the centuries, we might begin by asking, "As a matter of interest, what were *you* doing inside the house of Simon the Pharisee? How did you get past the door?"

We can imagine her reply. "That was easy. A dinner party in our day was like one of your cocktail parties where any number of invited and uninvited guests might come and go. Actually no one noticed me until I knelt down beside Jesus and began washing his feet."

"Wasn't that rather an unconventional thing to do?"

"It was impulsive," she admits, "and perhaps badly timed. I didn't stop to think how my presence might embarrass Jesus. He had performed a miracle in my life, and I couldn't wait to show him how grateful I was."

"Yes, but why express your gratitude in public before all those important people? Why not thank Jesus privately?"

"My thanksgiving *had* to be a public gesture," she explains. "You see, I was a public figure. Everybody knew me or, at least, they knew who I was. So I wanted everyone to know what had happened to me. Especially I wanted the Pharisees to know."

We admire the woman for her courage and we wonder what inspired it. "You say that Jesus performed a miracle in your life. What was that miracle?"

"He forgave my sins," she replies simply.

That doesn't seem unusual. Across the pages of the Gospels there walks a long procession of men and women whose sins Jesus forgave, yet none of them offered such impulsive and extravagant gestures of gratitude. We point this out to her. "Perhaps not," she says. "But my case was different. You have to remember the sort of person that I was. The New Testament delicately describes me as 'a woman who was living an immoral life'. Your modern novels, with their four-letter words, would call me a whore."

Looking at her now, we could not be more astonished if the confession came from the lips of a Roman Catholic nun or a Salvation Army girl. This woman has beauty in her face, refined beauty like gold purified in fire. Remembering the rigid code of Jewish society, we boldly ask, "Why were you not stoned to death?"

Her voice carries a faint tone of bitterness. "Because I was not married. And that should tell you something about our moral codes and the unliberated status of woman in our first century world. An adulterous wife was punished not for her immorality but for her infidelity. She belonged to one man in the same way that his fields and cattle belonged to him. As an item of her husband's property she came under the laws of property. A harlot belonged to all men. She was considered beneath the moral code, even beneath animals."

This is obviously a woman to whom we can talk frankly; so, even though it sounds naïve, we ask the next question: "You say that you were a prostitute. That must have been an unpleasant existence!"

She shuts her eyes as though to ease her tortured memory. "It was sheer hell!" she whispers. Then, after a pause, "It's bad enough to let yourself get entangled in a fleeting love affair or to distribute your affections too freely, but to be a person who makes a business of sex, selling your body to men whom you neither love nor respect — you can't sink lower than that!"

"We take it, then, that you were pretty much a social outcast."

"That," she replies, "is putting it mildly. When I walked down the road, good people crossed to the other side. Mothers stood in front of their chidren to prevent them from seeing me. Pharisees gathered their priestly robes as though the very dust on which I walked would contaminate them. Roman soldiers leered lecherously and made vulgar jokes. I had no friends. Women shunned me. Even my male patrons, when I met them on the street next day, looked right through me as though I were a total stranger. Their hypocrisy sickened me."

"Yet something changed you. What was it? Were you ashamed of being a prostitute?"

"I pretended not to be," she replies honestly. "Oh, my conscience bothered me at first. I used to promise myself that this thing would not go on forever, each time would be the last, some day I should meet a man who would care for me and say 'Let me take you away from all of this.' But soon I realised that I had gone too far for that. Who would ever respect me as a person again? I had reached the point of no return, so I tried not to think about it any more."

"Yet you did change. What made you do it?"

We can read the answer in her face which takes on a

radiance that wipes away all traces of bitterness and tortured memory. She says simply, "I did meet a man who cared for me and took me away from it all."

"You mean that you met Jesus?"

The woman looks at us with astonishment. "How can you speak that name so easily? Yes, I met Jesus one day on a narrow street. 'My next customer,' I thought; but before I could give him the usual invitation, he said, 'Excuse me,' and stepped down into the donkey gutter to let me pass. I thought he must be poking fun at me, because no one had treated me that politely for a long time. Then I looked into his eyes. There was no fun in them, only a kind of sadness, as though he knew the woman I was and felt sorry about it. He smiled courteously and walked on."

"Of course, you didn't know who he was."

"Not then, but I soon found out. It seems that Jesus spent a lot of time talking to my sort of people and trying to help them. That's why the religious leaders had no use for him. After that I always seemed to be running into him. Not that I wanted to. God knows I hated him at first, because the very sight of him awakened within me feelings which I thought were dead."

"You could have avoided him," we suggest.

"Can you avoid him?" she asks pointedly. "I tried to but I couldn't. He had started a fire inside me and left it raging out of control. All of a sudden I felt dirty. I hated my harlotry. I began making excuses to the men who wanted me to go with them, and that was risky, because I depended on them for a living. When I told them the reason, some of them laughed; others got angry and threatened to have me arrested and stoned. It didn't matter, though. Jesus had shown me that I was sick in my soul, and I couldn't avoid him because I felt sure that only he could cure me."

"What exactly do you mean?" we ask her.

She replies, "I mean that Jesus was different from other men, cleaner, nobler and kinder. Sometimes he didn't seem like a man at all. He seemed more like God. He talked about God and left you with the idea that he knew what he was talking about. He did things that only God could do. He made blind people see and lame people walk and bad people good. He was so good himself and so happy about it that he made you want to be like him. 'Your sins are forgiven' — that's what he said to some of the worst people; and suddenly I knew that more than anything else in the world I wanted him to say it to me. I felt sure that if Jesus forgave my sins, God would forgive them too."

We remark that it seems rather marvellous that a woman of the streets should recognise in Jesus what many respectable and religious people, like Simon the Pharisee, failed to recognise.

"I don't think so," she replies modestly. "Extremes always react to each other. Evil may wreck your life but at least it is real. The trouble with some respectable and religious people is that they live in a world of unreality. Their own good can blind them to the best."

Those words make us feel uncomfortable. They come embarrassingly close to describing our own condition, so we side-track the issue by saying, "You raise an interesting question. What was Jesus doing at Simon's house anyway? Didn't the Pharisees generally ostracise him?"

The woman smiles knowingly as she replies, "Don't let Simon's hospitality deceive you. It was nothing but a bid for social prominence. You see, by this time Jesus had become the talk of the town, something of a celebrity, at least among the poorer classes; and Simon probably thought it would be entertaining to have him as a guest in his home. You can imagine the conversation at the Temple that led up to it. One of the Pharisees would ask, 'Simon, what do you know about this Jesus?' Simon would answer, 'Not a great deal, but I tell you what I'll do. I'll give a dinner party for him. He will be flattered, and we shall have an opportunity to see him for ourselves'."

"But Jesus was not flattered?"

"No indeed. He came to the feast with his eyes wide open and he didn't miss a thing. He saw right away that his host extended to him none of the usual courtesies — the kiss of greeting, the water for his feet and the oil for his head. He sensed the situation but said nothing about it until I appeared on the scene and began doing for him the very things that Simon had deliberately neglected to do. Then

Jesus turned the tables on him. 'Simon,' he said in a voice that everyone could hear, 'I have something to say to you.' 'What is it, Teacher?' asked Simon innocently, but he regretted giving Jesus a chance to speak, because what Jesus said made Simon appear unforgivably boorish and humiliated him before all the guests."

Our next question sounds harsh but it is the crucial question that unlocks the secret place of this woman's soul and brings us back to the heart of the matter. "You say that you felt sure that if Jesus forgave your sins, God would forgive them. Considering how degraded your life had been, wasn't that expecting rather a lot of God?"

Again we can read agony in her face as she says, "I didn't expect anything of God. I had no right to. The truth is that for a long time I hadn't even thought about God. I dared not think about him. But I was sure of this: if God ever thought about me, it was with thoughts of anger. I had been brought up to believe that God will make us pay for every sin that we commit, and I knew that if I lived a thousand years I could never pay for my sins. Before his justice I stood condemned for all eternity."

"What changed your mind?"

"Jesus did," she replies. "As I told you, he seemed to be like God. I couldn't figure him out at first. 'Who is this man?' I kept asking myself. 'Who is this manly man with the strong body of a soldier and the gentle face of an angel?' The more I saw him and heard him preach and watched him perform miracles, the more I thought that if there is a God in heaven he must be like Jesus. And I knew that if God is like Jesus, I needn't be afraid of him any more. I could pray to him again and tell him about myself. He wouldn't be angry. He would understand."

"So you went to Jesus and told him."

"Yes."

"And he forgave you?"

"He did."

"Do you want to talk about it?"

"Not really. There are some things you cannot easily talk about, things so personal, so terrible or so wonderful that they make no sense to people who have never experienced them. I can only tell you this: I went to Jesus and told him *everything*, every detail of my life in the gutter. I didn't hold back a thing. I recited the whole sordid story from beginning to end. I felt sure that Jesus would turn his back and walk disgustedly away. Instead, he listened as if he had been expecting me ever since that day when I met him on the street and as if he knew more about me than I knew about myself. There was sternness in his eyes; it pierced my heart like a knife, but a sternness full of understanding and pity."

"And you took that to mean that God had forgiven you — just like that? Cancelled your sins? Erased the past? Wiped the slate clean?"

"You are not being serious," she replies. "You wouldn't respect a God who cancelled with a word all the harm that you have done to yourself and others. I knew that my sins would haunt me for the rest of my days. I could never forget them. People would not allow me to forget. They would still cross to the other side of the street, still shield their children's eyes. They would judge me for what I had been, not for what I became. Their hearts are not as big as the heart of Christ. But it didn't matter. I could take any human punishment now. All that mattered when I left the presence of Jesus that day was that God had forgiven me and that my life as a harlot had come to an end."

"So that is why you crashed Simon's party and made a public spectacle of yourself?"

"Surely you see that I had to do it," she replies excitedly. "In the days that followed I was delirious with joy. I felt like a condemned criminal suddenly released from a dark dungeon. I was pardoned! Free! I wanted to shout it from the rooftops. I wanted everyone to know and understand what had happened to me."

"But Simon didn't understand?"

"No. My whole performance disgusted Simon. Jesus tried to explain by telling him about the two debtors, one of whom owed a man fifty pieces of silver and the other five hundred pieces, how the creditor cancelled both debts and how the larger debtor would have more cause to be grateful. Pointing to me, Jesus said to Simon, 'I tell you, her great love proves that her many sins have been forgiven; where little has been forgiven, little love is shown.' The story was wasted on Simon. He had no sense of indebtedness to Jesus. He didn't owe Jesus anything. He believed that Jesus owed him something."

"Were you sorry, then, that you tried to make him understand?"

"I was sorry for him but not for myself. I think that Jesus appreciated all that I did for him that day. As the servants grabbed my arm and started to shove me out into the street where they thought I belonged, Jesus looked straight at me and said something that opened the door of heaven, 'Your faith has saved you; go in peace.' "

For a moment we feel tongue-tied. We can think of nothing more to say to this remarkable woman who has shown us the secret place of her soul and taken us into the very heart of the Gospel. Do we understand her any better than Simon did? Do we understand Jesus any better than Simon did? We cannot leave her without asking one more question, "Why did you anoint the feet of Jesus with expensive ointment, your only remaining possession of any material value after you had renounced your means of earning a livelihood? Why such costly devotion?"

She stares at us incredulously. "Then you don't understand. But how could you. As Jesus said — it's only when you are forgiven much that you love much. You see, when Christ has given you everything, when you have been dead and he has brought you to life and made you a new person with a new hope, a new opportunity and a new future, you want to give everything back to him."

CHAPTER NOTES:

1.   Mark 14:3-9; Matt. 26:6-13; Luke 7:36-50; John 12:1-8

IV

These Opposed Him

13
Caiaphas

The Powerful Priest

IN THE NUREMBERG war trials civilised nations reckoned seriously for the first time with the whole concept of corporate guilt. Former officers of the Hitler regime were tried and sentenced not for the crimes which they had personally committed but for the larger and more brutal crimes which they had conceived and directed.

Suppose it were possible to bring to a similar trial the men who crucified Jesus. For sheer criminality nothing surpasses that infamous deed committed in Palestine over a twelve-hour period nearly two thousand years ago. The Cross still ranks as one of the grimmest atrocities of the human race. History has judged the men responsible, heaped its contempt upon them and cast them out into the utter darkness of shame and scorn. But what if we could actually bring them to trial, just as we brought the Nazis at Nuremberg, judging them not as individuals but as a group corporately accused of committing a foul and heinous crime against the human race?

Silence falls on the courtroom as the defendants, looking like the cast of characters in a Good Friday television drama, rise to hear the charge laid against them: "...did wilfully premeditate and on the morning of Friday...in the year of our Lord 29 carry out and execute the murder of one Jesus of Nazareth... Do you plead guilty or not guilty?"

No single one of the defendants — Caiaphas, Pilate, Judas, the Roman Centurion or any of the others — would himself plead guilty. Judged only on the basis of his own share in the Calvary episode, he might reasonably plead innocence and in the end be acquitted. But remember: these men are being judged for their corporate guilt. While each is not the whole jig-saw puzzle, each fits like a piece into the jig-saw puzzle, and the picture is not complete without him. A murder has been committed, a crime which might never have taken place unless each man now standing in the prisoners' dock had played his particular part. We have to determine their relative guilt.

We begin with Caiaphas because we have no difficulty establishing his guilt. If any one man can be singled out as being responsible for the crucifixion of Jesus, it was Joseph Caiaphas, the High Priest of the temple of Jerusalem. It was he who instigated the arrest of Jesus, he who paid Judas the thirty pieces of silver, he who presided over the kangaroo trial, he who presented the charges to Pilate, he of whom Jesus said to Pilate, "the deeper guilt lies with the man who handed me over to you".[1] Caiaphas was the brains behind Calvary; all the others were tools in his hand. He conceived, plotted and engineered the whole sordid affair. He was the real villain of the Good Friday drama.

Take a look at this man who held the highest and holiest office in ancient Israel. He seems impressive in his priestly robes, though they do not hide the smugness of his face and the calculated cunning in his eyes. Beyond any doubt he was the most powerful man in the Jewish nation, the classic example of a worldly ecclesiastic whose influence reached far beyond the house of God, a first century Cardinal Richelieu. As High Priest he exercised spiritual power. He was the closest thing to a pope, the primate of the established religion, who held in his hand the keys of the Kingdom of Heaven. He alone could enter the Holy of Holies in the temple at Jerusalem. It was through him that the whole nation came to God and found forgiveness for its sins.

Caiaphas was economically powerful too. He had some 20,000 priests working for him in the temple, and they all took their wages every week. They were paid not from voluntary offerings but from the taxes of the people. Every Jew, in addition to being taxed by the government in Rome, had to pay taxes to the temple in Jerusalem. It was a lucrative enterprise. In fact, there is no source of revenue more profitable than taxation, and Caiaphas operated his own tax system which included all Jews in the Mediterranean world. A High Priest soon became a wealthy man.

His principal power was political. He received his office by appointment of Rome — which is not unlike an Archbishop today being appointed by the Prime Minister of a secular government. For several years a single family had monopolised the office of High Priest. Caiaphas, who held it for fourteen years, succeeded his father-in-law, Annas. As an appointee of Rome he became the stool-pigeon of Rome, a pipeline of information to the Emperor's ear. Pontius Pilate discovered that to his chagrin. On at least three occasions he had the bad sense to tangle with Caiaphas, which resulted in costly blunders for which he was reprimanded by Caesar. He knew where Caesar got his information. As Roman Governor Pilate soon learned that he was not the most powerful man in Judea. Caiaphas was the real power, and Pilate hated and feared him.

He Gave the Orders

A man who enjoys that much power is not likely to tolerate someone who threatens it, even though that person is a good man and a loyal citizen. The conflict with Jesus was inevitable. Caiaphas did not object to his going about and doing good but he did object to what Jesus said, the ideas that he put into people's heads, the danger that he might stir them up to revolt. He particularly objected to the ridiculous rumours that the man might be the Messiah. In our reverence for the memory of Martin Luther King, the great apostle of non-violence, we are surprised that many people regarded him as a dangerous man; they believed that he fanned in people's minds the fires of racial discontent that later blazed out in violent action. Caiaphas opposed Jesus for the same reason. On one occasion he sent the temple police to arrest him. When they returned empty-handed, he demanded, "Why have you not brought him?" They replied, "No man ever spoke as this man speaks." There was little tolerance or love in what the priests said to that.[2]

You can be sure that after that incident Caiaphas planted

his spies in every crowd that surrounded Jesus wherever he went. Then two things happened that brought his opposition to a swift climax. The first was the raising of Lazarus from the dead.[3] That really worried the priests. It was one thing to convert a few prostitutes and cure a few cripples, but a man who could raise the dead could as easily raise a revolution. Hurriedly they convened a meeting of the Council. "What action are we taking?" they said. "This man is performing many signs. If we leave him alone like this the whole populace will believe in him. Then the Romans will come and sweep away our temple and our nation." Crafty Caiaphas was a step ahead of them. "Obviously the man must die," he said, in effect, "otherwise our nation will die." He actually said with his usual suave superiority, "You know nothing whatever; you do not even use your judgment; it is more to your interest that one man should die for the people, than that the whole nation should be destroyed."[4] We have to assume that Caiaphas did, in fact, care for the nation, though we assume also that he cared for his prestigious and profitable role in the nation. He could adroitly hide his own self-interest under the cloak of patriotism. At any rate, the fateful decision had been made; all that remained to be settled was the date.

That was quickly decided when the second event happened. The occasion was Passover Week, the most important week of the year to the priests, and the most profitable. During that week the pilgrims came in their hundreds to offer the required sacrifices in the temple. Each had to pay the temple tax which by today's values amounted to more than a dollar. All foreign money had to be changed in the temple, at a twenty per cent commission, into Galilean currency which alone was acceptable to the temple traders who had a monopoly on the birds and animals required for the sacrifices. The whole place must have looked and smelled like an agricultural fair. Only the priets knew how staggering was the revenue from this annual rip-off; and heaven help the man who dared to upset it. Jesus dared to upset it. On the Monday of the Passover Week he burst like a bomb-shell into this stronghold of the priests where they thought they had everything under control. He drove out the traders, kicked over the tables of the money-changers, sent the birds and animals flying in all directions and shouted, "Scripture says, 'My house shall be called a house of prayer', but you are making it a robbers' cave."[5]

You can just hear the priests exploding, "That does it! Caiaphas was right! The man must die!" It didn't take long for them to assemble at the High Priest's house and begin laying plans for the arrest and death of Jesus.[6] But they had one problem, and even Caiaphas was not sure how to deal with it. Jesus was a popular hero, and the temple incident had only heightened his popularity. If they seized him in broad daylight during the festival, the people would riot, and that was exactly what they wanted to prevent. If only they knew where he went every night they could arrest him quickly and quietly and have him sentenced and crucified while people were still in their beds. Suddenly the solution fell like manna from heaven. Judas Iscariot, one of the disciples of Jesus, came before the Council and said, "What will you give me to betray him to you?" "They weighed out for him thirty pieces of silver."[7]

Only two more obstacles stood between Caiaphas and the liquidation of his enemy. Having arrested Jesus, he couldn't just murder the man. He must have him convicted and executed by the due process of the law. That meant a trial before the Sanhedrin, the Jewish Parliament, a religious court that could find the prisoner to be worthy of death. The charge had to be blasphemy. Caiaphas arranged for a quorum of the Sanhedrin to be ready and waiting when the soldiers brought Jesus from the Garden of Gethsemane. At first the court could not find sufficient evidence to warrant the death sentence, but Caiaphas took care of that by introducing some witnesses whom he had carefully coached. A modern writer has counted forty-three such flagrant illegalities in the arrest, trial and execution of Jesus. For a while Caiaphas seemed beaten by the silence of Jesus, who refused to answer any of his questions, and he feared that his victim might slip between his fingers. Then, drawing his priestly robes about him, he threw a question that Jesus had to answer or deny all his claims: "By the living God I charge you to tell us: are you the Messiah, the Son of God?" At Jesus' answer the High

Priest, affecting pious horror, tore his robes and shouted,
"Blasphemy!" — to which the Sanhedrin roared, "He is
guilty...he should die."[8]

The remaining obstacle was Pontius Pilate, the Roman
Governor of Judea, who alone had the authority to pass the
death sentence. Pilate, with his Roman sense of justice, might
see through the priestly plot, he might find the prisoner
innocent and refuse to convict him. Certainly he hated
Caiaphas and would do anything to make him appear a fool.
However, the master manipulator had taken care of that too.
Late on Thursday night, even before Jesus was arrested,
Caiaphas probably went to see the Governor, waved a few
threats in front of his face and told him what was expected of
him next morning. There is also a theory that he stirred up a
great deal of advance sympathy for Barabbas, so that there
was nothing spontaneous about the crowd's choice of that
criminal over Jesus.

Clever, cunning Caiaphas showed his consummate crafti-
ness in the way he handled Pilate during the trial and in his
manipulation of the crowd. In the statement of charges he
carefully began with the civil offence: "We found this man
subverting our nation, opposing the payment of taxes to
Caesar, and claiming to be Messiah, a king."[9] When Pilate,
after examining Jesus, declared that he could find no case
against him, the priests insisted, "His teaching is causing
disaffection among the people all through Judea."[10] Pilate
tried to extricate himself with honour but he knew right from
the start that the priests had him cornered. How could he
acquit the prisoner without seeming to connive at treason and
insurrection, thereby jeopardising his career and possibly his
life? Sensing their victory, the priests played their final trump
card when they shouted at the Roman Governor before all the
people, "If you let this man go, you are no friend to Caesar."[11]

Exit Caiaphas from the Gospel drama. We don't see him
on stage again, though we do recognise his fine hand
manipulating some of the subsequent events. On his instructions, or at least with his blessing, the priests clustered around
the cross and joined the spectators in jeering at Jesus.[12] On
his instructions a deputation of priests went to Pilate on
Saturday morning and requested that a guard be stationed at

the sepulchre in case the disciples stole the body of Jesus and then told people that he had risen from the dead. "You may have your guard," said Pilate; "go and make it secure as best you can."[13] But how secure can man make anything against the power of God? On Easter Day we see the hand of Caiaphas again bribing the soldiers to spread the ridiculous rumour about the empty tomb: "His disciples came by night and stole the body while we were asleep."[14]

The Sin of Self-Interest

However we judge the other defendants in the war-crimes trial, we have no reasonable doubt that the High Priest Caiaphas stands guilty as charged. Guilty of what? What was his real sin? Of what does he stand accused before the bar of heaven? Older translations of the Bible use the word "expediency", quoting his classic statement to the Council, "...it is expedient for you that one man should die for the people, and that the whole nation should not perish."[15] The dictionary defines expedience as "the subordination of moral principles for the sake of attaining the desired end", a definition that fits the character of Caiaphas like a glove. Yet the New English Bible comes closer to the core of his guilt by translating his words, "...it is more to your interest that one man should die for the people, than that the whole nation should be destroyed". Certainly it was in Caiaphas' own interest that Jesus should die. If Jesus were allowed to live, being what he was and what he claimed to be, Caiaphas the High Priest might soon be out of a job.

Self-interest has always been the sin that crucified Christ or at least tried to smother him. Out of sheer political self-interest King Herod the Great tried to murder him in his cradle.[16] Out of sheer economic self-interest the British Parliament tried to frustrate the early missionary enterprises and stifle every effort to export the Gospel to its colonies. Out of sheer ideological self-interest the Communists have closed churches, persecuted priests, ridiculed religion and penalised the faithful. The Caiaphas-mentality is quite common and is considered a workable philosophy, perhaps the only workable philosophy of life. Self-interest is the great motivating force in politics, business, industry, labour relations, diplomacy, communications; it is the secret of wealth and success and power. It also keeps Christ on his Cross.

The sin of self-interest lies at the root of many of the world's problems today. The spectre of hunger haunts the human race, and we are urged to share with the needy nations, but we feel a sense of futility when we see them spending bread money on bombs. We see the ridiculous spectacle of starving peoples poised to fight and annihilate each other and we ask, Why does the poor world spend its limited resources on weapons? The answer is another question — Why is the rich world so anxious to supply them and lend the money to buy them? We know that ninety per cent of the Third World's major weapons imports come from the major powers. We know that some countries actually initiate the sales of armaments to poor countries in order to finance their own defence spending and arms industries. We know also that countries which provide weapons to the Third World free of charge do so in order to advance their own political, economic and ideological interests. George Bernard Shaw asked in one of his plays, "Must a Christ perish in every age to save those who have no imagination?" The answer is Yes, so long as men and nations succumb to the sin of self-interest.

Friedrich Deurrenmatt's play, *The Visit*, [17] tells the story of a small town in Europe which has gone economically bankrupt. Only one person can save it from extinction, and she is a fabulously rich woman who left the community many years before and plans to return for a visit. No one suspects that it was actually she who bought the industries and closed them down and put people out of work and caused the town to go bankrupt. She arrives with her weird entourage, she offers to put the town on its feet again and she stipulates her price. It must be the life of the leading citizen who made her pregnant and deserted her when she was a girl. The town fathers are shocked by her criminally insane demand. Murder a man? Do you think we are barbarians? Gradually, however, their thinking changes; and one after another the various segments of society — the law, the school, business, the town council, the Church, even the man's family — decide that one person's life is not an unreasonable price to pay for the common good. In the end they kill him. It is a devastating commentary on human nature and a powerful commentary on the Scripture text, "...it is more to your interest that one man should die for the people, than that the whole nation should be destroyed."

Caiaphas is not only an historical figure. He is every man, every nation, every government, every institution, every Church that will crucify God's Christ to preserve its own self-interest. One thing Caiaphas is not. He is not a High Priest. A priest is a mediator. He represents man to God and God to man. He stands like a human bridge between man and God. In his person man and God meet. Caiaphas was never that in anything but name only. Caiaphas himself needs a high priest, one who will take his sins to God and find forgiveness for them and reconcile him to the great heart of truth and justice and love. Christ is that High Priest. Caiaphas made him so when he put him on the Cross. The Apostle Paul pictures him in his priestly role when he takes us into another courtroom and asks, "Who will be the accuser of God's chosen ones? It is God who pronounces acquittal; then who can condemn?" He answers, "It is Christ who died, and, more than that, was raised from the dead — who is at God's right hand, and indeed pleads our cause." [18]

CHAPTER NOTES:

1. John 19:11
2. John 7:32-52
3. John 11:17-44
4. John 11:47-52
5. Matt. 21:12-13
6. Matt. 26:3-5
7. Matt. 26:14-16
8. Matt. 26:59-66
9. Luke 23:2
10. Luke 23:5
11. John 19:12
12. Mark 15:32
13. Matt. 27:62-66
14. Matt. 28:13
15. John 11:50 (R.S.V.)
16. Matt. 2:16-18
17. Published in Toronto by Random House Ltd.
18. Romans 8:33-34

14
Judas Iscariot

My Name

MY NAME IS Judas Iscariot. In all the Gospels I am listed last among the disciples as "the man who betrayed him".[1] That's how history remembers me. John said that I was a thief,[2] and Jesus himself called me a devil.[3]

Yet there is nothing sinister about my name. "Iscariot" simply means "son of Kerioth" or "citizen of Kerioth", and that's important because it tells you that I came from Kerioth, a small village south of Jerusalem in the region where the prophet Amos was born. "Judas" is a good name, or was until I made it a synonym for treachery. It means "praise of God". My parents rejoiced when I was born and gave thanks to God. They named me after the most famous military leader in our history, Judas Maccabeus. So you see, I made a good start. I was brought up in a religious home and taught to love and honour my people, my country and my God.

Maybe you're not interested in hearing my story. That suits me fine. I'd like nothing better than to crawl back into the woodwork of history and be left permanently alone, but the trouble is that people won't leave me alone. They keep dragging me out and scrutinising me as they would scrutinise a stuffed rattlesnake. "Poor old Judas. So long Judas." That couplet comes from one of your rock operas which has made a few million dollars for the boys who wrote it. They called it *Jesus Christ Superstar*,[4] but it's wrongly named, because Jesus doesn't have the best lines and songs. He doesn't have the leading role. I do. I am the real star of *Superstar*.

It's not a very reverent piece. It tells some truths about

Jesus but it doesn't really do him justice. It does justice to me, such as I deserve. Maybe the writers understand me better than they understand Jesus. They are right in supposing that I tried to advise Jesus. If he had taken my advice, things would have turned out differently — not to your benefit, perhaps, but differently. He refused to be guided by me, he let them crucify him, and that was the end of Judas Iscariot. But I'm getting ahead of my story. I'd like to tell it to you from the beginning, if you are willing to listen.

Right away I'd better let you know that I was the odd-man-out among the twelve disciples. I differed from the others in background, temperament and outlook. They came from Galilee; I came from Judea. They were country bumpkins; I was a city boy. They came from the labouring classes — fishermen, farmers, or carpenters like Jesus himself; I had some formal education and I had been around. I felt like a stranger among them, I couldn't get close to them, I didn't fit in. I felt lonely, misunderstood, unappreciated. That wouldn't have mattered if Jesus had appreciated my gifts. I could have been an asset to him. More than once I took him aside and quietly suggested that he take advantage of my knowledge and experience, but he shared his real confidence with those two hot-heads, James and John, and that loud-mouthed bluff, Peter. To me he said magnanimously, "Judas, you can be treasurer" Big deal! Treasurer, with no money in the bank!

My Hope

Why did I throw in my lot with Jesus at all? That can be answered simply. I have already told you that my parents gave me an illustrious name, a name which was once synonymous with patriotism, power and freedom. For five centuries my people had been no better than slaves. Never since the fall of Jerusalem in the fifth century B.C. had we known a single year of national independence. Only the brief rebellion led by my namesake, Judas Maccabeus, had broken for a moment the crippling yoke of slavery. Our country, when I was born, was an occupied country, a satellite province in the Roman Empire, bled white by taxes and terrorised by foreign soldiers who marched arrogantly through the streets. You would know what that meant if you lived today in some parts of Europe.

But I didn't give up hope. No indeed! I clung to a mighty hope which had beaten in the hearts of our people for generations, a hope which had kept them alive through all the indignity and suffering of conquest and slavery. Like every faithful Jew I looked for the coming of God's Messiah. I believed with all my soul in the promise of the great prophets that one day out of heaven would come an invincible Divine leader to rally our stricken people, crush our enemies into the dust and restore our national independence. I thought that Jesus was that heaven-sent leader. That's what the writers of *Superstar* don't understand about me. They've got me trying to persuade Jesus not to pose as the Messiah, whereas I really tried to persuade him to declare himself as the Messiah. At first I honestly believed him to be the Messiah. That's what attracted me to him, and that's why I threw in my lot with him.

Wouldn't you have done the same thing in my place? Jesus fitted the bill perfectly. He was a born leader, he had charisma. You couldn't keep the crowds away from him. From all over the country and beyond they flocked to hear him preach on the hillsides. And such preaching! No man ever spoke as authoritatively about God. And it wasn't only what he said about God. It was the way he brought the presence and power of God right into our experience just as the prophets had foretold that the Messiah would do. We had never seen anything like it before. He made blind men see and cripples walk. He cured lepers and insane people and even stopped a storm at the Sea of Galilee. Now I ask you—who else could he be but the Messiah?

All the time I kept thinking to myself, "One of these days he's going to tell us what we already know about him. One of these days the Prince disguised as a beggar is going to remove his disguise and take a sword in his hand." I thought the day had come when we stopped on the road to Caesarea Philippi, and Jesus asked who we thought he was. Peter answered for all of us, "You are the Messiah".[5] He didn't exactly admit it but neither did he deny it, and that was enough for me. I can't tell you how excited I felt in that moment. It was as though the great bell of freedom was about to ring. I could see it all so clearly. The end of oppression! Jerusalem the capital of the world! The nations, yes even Imperial Rome, doing homage to us! And to think that we twelve were in on the ground floor. What honour, what prestige would come to us, the cabinet ministers in the new Kingdom of Jesus! Don't get me wrong. I wasn't alone in that ambitious scheming. The others had it in mind too. It wasn't me, it was James and John who asked Jesus for their share of political plums.[6]

They asked him, and he said something about a cross. I couldn't figure that one out at all. In fact, I couldn't figure out a lot of things about Jesus. He had tacitly admitted to being the Messiah, but it didn't seem to make any difference to him. He just kept on doing what he had been doing before — healing beggars and blind men, lingering with losers and wasting his time with ones and twos. "This is ridiculous," I said to myself. "With all his power over the natural and supernatural why doesn't he sweep the Romans into the sea and restore the kingdom of our father, David? If he can raise the dead to life, why doesn't he raise up a revolution? He has only to raise his little finger, and all the young men in Palestine with red blood in their veins will rise up and follow him. Yet here he is fleeing like a fugitive with a handful of peasants, telling people to love one another, saying that he must suffer and babbling about a cross. That's no way for the Messiah to act." Then I began to suspect one of two things. Either he was not the Messiah, or else Messiahship meant for him something altogether different than we had expected. For us it meant dominion; for him, suffering. For us it meant violence; for him, non-violence. For us it meant a sword and a crown; for him, thorns and a Cross.

If I had been morally honest I should have walked out on him there and then. Yet I stayed, and you have to know Jesus to understand the reason why. The man had irresistible magnetism. Once you came under his spell you couldn't shake it off with a simple decision. Of course, my whole attitude to him changed. He sensed the change, he could read my thoughts of disappointment and disillusionment, he realised that I was falling away from him, yet he didn't change his attitude toward me. I disagreed with him, resented him, even hated him at times, yet he still loved me, still looked at me with those eyes of pity and pleading, as though to say, "Judas, Judas..." I would never have admitted it then, but I loved him too. Messiah or not, he was my friend, the best friend I ever had, and I betrayed his friendship.

You wonder how I could be so despicable. Well, let me explain that my patience broke during that last week in Jerusalem at the house of Simon the Leper. Until then I had not altogether given up hope that Jesus would declare himself before the whole nation as the true Messiah. My hopes came alive when he entered Jerusalem on Palm Sunday in a manner foretold by the prophets.[7] And imagine my excitement the next day when he strode into the temple court, kicked over the tables of the moneychangers and single-handed drove them all out like a flock of frightened geese.[8] That was my kind of Messiah. Things were beginning to move at last, and in the right direction. I really thought the moment had come two days later when a woman at Simon's house poured precious ointment over his head. I thought to myself, "Now he will come forward as the Lord's anointed." But do you know what he did? He turned the meaning of the act in a totally different direction by saying, "She has anointed my body beforehand for burying."[9] Think of it! She had offered a crown, and he had accepted a tomb.

My Scheme

That's when I formed my crazy, diabolical scheme that seemed so ingenious at the time. I decided that Jesus needed a push and that I ought to give it to him. I would force his hand, put him in a position where he had no choice but to exercise his Messianic power. It could be done very simply. Now that they had Jesus inside Jerusalem, the religious leaders were planning to arrest him and have him executed on some trumped-up charges; but they had to do it quietly and quickly, because Jesus was still popular with the people, and any attempt on his life would start a riot. If they could find out where Jesus went after dark every night they could seize him, try him, have him sentenced and crucified while most of the citizens were still in their beds. I went to the priests and offered to provide that information.[10] A friend of Jesus had given him the courtesy of a garden on the Mount of Olives during Passover week. I told the priests to go there.

They paid me thirty pieces of silver, and I accepted them. Why not? If Jesus were really the Messiah he would make fools of these priestly hypocrites. If not, I would save my skin and be richer in the process.

No don't get me wrong — sounds like *Superstar* — but understand this. Not for a moment did I suspect that my plan for Jesus would fail. After all, if a man can raise the dead to life he is not about to let people put him to death. Even in the Upper Room that Thursday evening I paid no attention to his vague talk about his body broken and blood shed. When he said those ominous words, "One of you will betray me," I wanted to shout out, "You won't call it betrayal when you see what happens. You'll be grateful for what I did." Why didn't I say it, then? Because I knew the truth, that's why. Your Gospels say that a devil entered my soul. Maybe it did — a devil of resentment and jealousy. For three years I had walked with Jesus, three precious years of my life wasted on the biggest loser of them all. He had made a fool of me, and I hated him for it, hated him for his soft talk, his stupid servility, his disgusting trick of washing our filthy feet. Oh God, why did he have to wash my feet? Why did he have to look at me and whisper, "Do it quickly, Judas"? Yes, a devil entered my soul, and for just a moment I wanted Jesus to die. If he were not the Messiah but only another pretender, the sooner we got rid of him the better. So I left the Upper Room, scarcely noticed by the others who, had they suspected where I was going, would forcibly have held me back. A couple of hours later I guided the soldiers to the Garden of Gethsemane.

But you've got to believe me when I say again that I did not expect Jesus to be arrested in Gethsemane. Why else would I have behaved as I did after his arrest? I can still see that incredulous look on the faces of the disciples when they saw me at the head of the goon squad. "Judas," they seemed to say, "how could you do it?" Then I kissed Jesus, as a disciple greets his rabbi, to identify him to the soldiers. And do you know what he said with my traitorous kiss still hot on his cheek? "Friend, do what you are here to do."[12] It was the last name by which he ever addressed me — "friend". As the soldiers moved forward, everything within me screamed, "Now! Now! Strike them dead now!" Even the other disciples wanted to fight it out, but Jesus stopped them and said, "God can give me twelve legions of angels." "Well, for God's sake, call the twelve legions of angels! Call one angel!" But he didn't call anyone. The soldiers took him, and he went with them as meek as a lamb. My brilliant scheme had failed.

My Tragedy

Then I was alone. Even the devil wasn't around any more. I stood there in the garden, dazed by the dreadful thought of the terrible events which I had set in motion. They had to be stopped somehow. I must tell the soldiers that they had made an awful mistake. They mustn't go through with this thing. Jesus was not a revolutionary. He had done nothing to deserve death. He mustn't die. If he died, I could never look myself in the face again. Like a crazy man I rushed out of the garden, across the Kedron Valley, through the city gate, up and down the streets, knocking on doors all night long to find someone with influence who might help me to rescue Jesus. But it was too late. The priests had their victim in a cage and they were preparing to slaughter him. Not much chance that they would listen to me, but I was desperate. I forced my way into their council chamber just as the soldiers were taking Jesus to Pontius Pilate to be sentenced. I gave them back their rotten money and shouted, "I have brought an innocent man to his death." They weren't even interested. "That's your problem," they said.[13]

There are two theories about what happened to me after that. One says that I went out and hanged myself and that the priests, when they heard of it, used the blood money to buy a field as a burial place for strangers which they fittingly called "Blood Acre".[14] The other says that I bought Blood Acre with the tainted money and there met with a gruesome fatal accident.[15] Take your pick. They add up to the same thing. Either way my life had become intolerable, my mind unhinged, and the sight of myself despicable. How could I live any longer in a world made decent and friendly by the presence of Jesus? He and I could never be together in the same place again. The Bible says that I abandoned the apostleship to ho to my own place (Acts 1:25) — the only place in God's universe where I belonged. From that place I speak to you now.

Do you think that I over-reacted by committing suicide? Was betrayal such a big crime compared to the hypocrisy of Caiaphas, the cowardice of Pilate, the brutality of the executioners? Perhaps not, but then none of them had ever known Jesus. I walked with him for three years, heard his sermons, saw his miracles, listened to his prayers. He chose me along with Peter and John and the others to be with him and proclaim his Gospel and share his ministry among men. There is no sin worse than this — to be with Jesus and completely misunderstand him; then, because you cannot accept his way above your own, to betray him with hot, bitter, cruel, impatient pride.

One of the church fathers had another theory about me. He suggested that I committed suicide so that I might meet Jesus in Hades, the world of the dead, and implore his forgiveness. I could have done that without taking my life, and that's my ultimate tragedy. I could have fled to Jesus that very night while he was still alive. I could have rushed to him wherever he was — in the court of the High Priest, the judgment hall of Pilate or even on the Cross — and flung myself at his feet. What matter if the soldiers had cut me down? I know that Jesus would have forgiven me. He forgives every man who betrays him and is truly sorry for his betrayal. The road that leads to the great heart of God in Christ is never closed by day or by night, in life or in death.

CHAPTER NOTES

1. Mark 3;19; Matt. 10:4
   Luke 6:15
2. John 12:16
3. John 6:70-71
4. Copyright 1970 by
   Leeds Music Ltd., London.
5. Mark 8:27ff.
6. Mark 10:35ff.
7. Matt. 21:1ff.
8. Mark 11:15-19
9. Mark 14:3-9
10. Mark 14:10
11. John 13:1-30
12. Matt. 26:47-56
13. Matt. 27:3-4
14. Matt. 27:6-10
15. Acts 1:18-20

15
Pilate

Give Pilate a Fair Deal

THERE WAS NOTHING fanciful about the suggestion in a previous chapter that the crucifiers of Jesus be put on trial. In October 1974, a civil court in France was asked to fix the blame for the crucifixion of Jesus on Pontius Pilate, the Roman governor of Judea, and thereby absolve the Jewish people of their collective guilt. The plaintiff was a lawyer named Jacques Isorni who in 1967 published a book entitled *The True Trial of Jesus*, maintaining that Jesus was condemned and crucified under Roman law as an alleged leader of guerrilla warfare against the Roman occupation, and not because he claimed to be the Son of God.[1]

The Church has been blaming Pilate for two thousand years. Every time a Christian congregation stands up and recites the Apostles' Creed it singles out Pilate as the villain of the Good Friday drama, as though he alone were responsible for the injustice and atrocity of that most infamous event. "I believe in... Jesus Christ...born of the Virgin Mary, suffered under Pontius Pilate..." Why Pilate? Why not Caiaphas, the High Priest, of whom Jesus himself said to Pilate, "...the deeper guilt lies with the man who handed me over to you"?[2] Perhaps it is time we gave Pilate a fair deal. To be sure, he sentenced Jesus to death but did he have any other choice? What would you have done in his place?

That might be a different and fascinating way to study the character of Pilate. Try to imagine yourself in his place. Travel back two thousand years, step inside his sandals and see yourself playing his role in the Good Friday drama. It is the year A.D. 26. You are a Roman career diplomat, a man about the same age as Jesus, and you have just been appointed Governor of Judea and Jerusalem. You have mixed feelings about the appointment. You know that the Jews are the most difficult of all Caesar's subjects to govern, yet you know also that if you can do the job well and avoid the errors of your predecessors, your future in Caesar's service will be assured. It is a tough one, but so are you; and if firm measures are required, you are determined to take them.

From the moment you step on Judean soil everything goes wrong. You just haven't reckoned with the stubborn Jews and their fanatical worship of one God and their hatred of oppression and their secret contempt for the Roman Empire. Especially you haven't reckoned with Caiaphas, their crafty High Priest. Your predecessor appointed him, but you can't remove him, because he has cleverly insinuated himself into the good graces of Caesar. The man actually has more power than you have, and more cunning. He frustrates you at every turn. First you try a display of power. You order your soldiers to carry images of the Emperor into the Jewish temple. Caiaphas promptly orders two thousand praying Jews to surround your palace for six days and nights until you threaten to massacre them, and then they bare their necks and dare you to do it. Enraged and humiliated, you order the images taken down. Then you try a benevolent approach. Jerusalem needs a fresh water supply, so you decide to build an aqueduct, which pleases the Jews, but you make the mistake of financing it from their temple treasury. They start a riot, your soldiers put it down, there are some deaths, and you get a scathing rebuke from the Emperor.

So it continues until Caiaphas and his crowd have you over a barrel. You don't rule them; they rule you. By the time history links your name with that of Jesus you are a frightened, insecure man, knowing that if you make any more mistakes, and Caesar hears about them, you're through. You have heard of Jesus of Nazareth. Who hasn't? Your wife, Claudia Procula, an intelligent and cultured woman whose judgment you trust, speaks highly of him. He seems to be a harmless enough person. He apparently goes about with a little group of disciples teaching people to love one another, even their enemies; he helps them in their troubles and cures their illnesses. He could be a stabilising influence in the country. You know that the priests take a dim view of Jesus but you have no idea that they are plotting his death.

You learn that from Caiaphas on the Thursday evening of Passover Week. Usually you reside in Caesarea but you always move to Jerusalem during the great Jewish festivals sso that you can be on the scene if God's chosen people become too patriotic and decide to revolt against Rome. Caiaphas comes to your official residence, the Tower of Antonia next to the temple, and tells you of the drama which is about to begin and of the part which he expects you to play in it. By midnight Jesus will be arrested, he will be tried immediately before the Jewish Sanhedrin and most certainly condemned to be worthy of death. Shortly after dawn he will be brought to your palace so that you may examine him and officially pass the death sentence. "Just a formality," says Caiaphas. "I think we understand each other." You understand right enough. You understand what will happen if you don't co-operate and Caiaphas sends one more report to Caesar. You don't get much sleep that night.

The Historic Trial

Next morning the priests are right on schedule. For fear of being made ritually unclean and therefore not being able to eat the Passover, they refuse to enter your house but demand that you come out to the balcony overlooking the courtyard.[3] You wish you had the courage to ignore their insulting demands. You step outside and survey them with contempt. Then you get your first sight of the prisoner in their midst, bound with chains, like a trussed-up lamb in a pack of wolves. You ask incredulously, "What charge do you bring against this man?" The priests retort angrily, "If he were not a criminal, we should not have brought him before you." Criminal indeed! You know where the crime really is and you are not going to be sucked into it. "Take him away and try him by your own law." They come back, "We are not allowed to put any man to death." You ask again, "What are the charges?" They specify three: "subverting the nation, opposing payment of taxes to Caesar, and claiming to be Messiah, a king".[4] An absurd fabrication! Any fool could see through it. But you had better go through the motions of giving the man a trial. You order him brought inside to your judgment hall.

So this is Jesus of Nazareth, the man they call king of the Jews! You study him for a moment and ask almost with amusement, "Are you the king of the Jews?"[5] You expect him to say, "Of course not!" but he answers with a question, an impertinent question, though he does not speak impertinently: "Is that your own idea, or have others suggested it to you?" That makes you angry. How dare he associate you with this whole hypocritical charade? "What! Am I a Jew? Your own nation and their chief priests have brought you before me. What have you done?" He replies, "My kingdom does not belong to this world. If it did, my followers would be fighting to save me from arrest by the Jews. My kingly authority comes from elsewhere." You wonder if the priests are right after all. Maybe this harmless-looking fellow does think that he is their Messiah. "You are a king, then?" He answers, " 'King' is your word. My task is to bear witness to the truth..." Truth! When did you ever hear the truth in a court of law? He tells you one thing, the priests tell you another. How do you know which to believe? "What is truth?" you exclaim cynically. However, you are sure of one thing: this man is no criminal. You really ought to acquit him and you know that you have it within your power to acquit him. All you have to do is summon a company of soldiers and clear the courtyard.

But will you do that and risk your reputation? Not if you can find a simpler and safer solution. The priests suggest one when you take Jesus outside and declare that you can find no case in him. They shout back, "His teaching is causing disaffection among the people all through Judea. It started from Galilee and has spread as far as this city".[6] There's the way out! The man is a Galilean, he comes under Herod's jurisdiction; and by happy coincidence Herod, the Tetrarch of Galilee, is in Jerusalem at this very moment. Let Herod try the case. That will get you off the hook very nicely. You send Jesus to him with your compliments. Herod thanks you for the compliment and sends Jesus back, dressed in a gorgeous robe. He refuses to do your dirty work for you. [7]

The ball is in your court again, but you are not unprepared for it. Another solution has suggested itself in the appearance of a different crowd of people clamouring for the Governor's annual Passover gift of clemency for a condemned Jewish prisoner.[8] They wouldn't appreciate it if you suddenly released a sabre-toothed tiger in their midst. In the dungeon there is a murderer named Barabbas who is as dangerous as any sabre-toothed tiger. The whole population breathed more easily when you locked him up, and nobody wants him on the loose again. He is public enemy number one. Why not make the crowd choose freedom either for him or for Jesus? They've got to choose Jesus. You step outside on the balcony and offer them the choice. Just then you are called inside to read an urgent message from your wife which says about Jesus, "Have nothing to do with that innocent man; I was much troubled on his account in my dreams last night." You are troubled right now and you are wide awake. That diversion gives the astute priests and rulers just enough time to circulate among the people, inciting them to demand the release of Barabbas and the death of Jesus. When you face them again and repeat the question, "Which of the two do you wish me to release to you?" they fling it in your teeth, "Barabbas!" You can't believe your ears. Falteringly you cry out, "Then what am I to do with Jesus called Messiah?"

Christ Was His Problem

Yes, Pontius Pilate, that's your problem, and it begins to look as though you're not going to be able to solve it. "What am I to do with Jesus called Messiah?" The crowd screams, "Crucify!" That's what they want you to do with him. You are about to give in when another idea crosses your mind, a brutal, inhuman idea, but at least it may save the man's life and your honour. You order the soldiers to take Jesus away and flog him.[9] He will be stripped naked, jeered at, insulted and flogged back and front by two strong men using a flagellum which is a multi-thonged whip made of ox-leather, knotted with small knuckle-bones or lead balls or even bronze hooks made to tear the flesh. He will be torn to pieces by the incessant blows and will look like a piece of chopped-up meat, if he survives at all. How can anyone desire his death after that? You can almost hear the retching sounds of people's stomachs as they catch sight of this broken, bloody figure in his crazy purple robe and crown of thorns. "Behold the Man!" you cry out with pity in your voice. But there is no pity in his accusers. "Crucify! Crucify!" they scream like animals thirsting for the kill. You shout at them, "Take him and crucify him yourselves; for my part I find no case against him." They shout back, "We have a law; and by that law he ought to die, because he has claimed to be the Son of God."

That frightens you, Pontius Pilate. You are not a religious man but you are superstitious, and that phrase "Son of God" sends shivers up and down your spine. You enter the judgment hall again, you summon the prisoner, you order your servants and soldiers to leave. You and he face each other, as though you were the only two men in the whole world. His calmness of spirit shakes your troubled soul, his fearlessness makes you feel like a cringing dog, his regality reduces you to the status of a slave. Why do you have an insane desire to stand up and salute him? Is he on trial before you, or are you on trial before him? Is he the Son of God? You've got to find out. "Where have you come from?" you ask him. He gives you no answer. You try to brazen it out. "Do you refuse to speak to me? Surely you know that I have authority to release you, and I have authority to crucify you?" As though calling your bluff he looks at you almost with an expression of pity and says through his excruciating pain, "You would have no authority at all over me, if it had not been granted to you from above; and therefore the deeper guilt lies with the man who handed me over to you." That's it! Now you know that you have to release him or you can never respect yourself again. You march out bravely to the people, but they know what you are going to say; and before you can open your mouth, they shout, "If you let this man go, you are no friend to Caesar; any man who claims to be a king is defying Caesar."

You are beaten and you know it. These clever priests have backed you into a corner. Adroitly they have put you in a position where you cannot administer justice without seeming to be guilty of treason; and that's a risk you dare not take.

Besides, even the people are growing restless over your continual hedging and are showing signs of a riot. [11] At last you make a futile gesture of washing your hands publicly, as though to protest your innocence of this man's blood, and then you hand him over to be crucified.

But you are as guilty as hell and you know it. Not even your other token gestures can wash away your guilt. Oh yes, you show your authority over that inscription for the cross, declaring categorically to the priests, "What I have written, I have written". [12] Without the usual financial consideration you give Joseph of Arimathea permission to take the body of Jesus down from the cross and bury it in his private sepulchre. [13] You provide the priests with a guard of soldiers for the sepulchre, saying to them, "...make it secure as best you can", probably adding under your breath, "...if you can." [14]

If Pilate Had Released Jesus

Thus Pilate played his role on the stage of history. If you had been in his place would you have played it differently and at what point would you have introduced changes into the scenario? Assuming that you saw through the hypocrisy of the man's accusers, would you simply have refused to try the case in the first place? Or having examined the prisoner and recognised his innocence, would you have acquitted him and put down any protest with a display of military force? Would you have taken a stand with Jesus, declaring to the priests and the crucifixion mob, "I am against you and for him; and if you try to crucify him you will have to kill me first"?

You know what would have happened after that. In the length of time that it takes for a ship to get to Rome the Emperor would have received a first-hand report of your conduct at the trial of Jesus, a report written in the ink of vitriolic hatred. In the time that it takes for a ship to get back to Caeserea you would have received an order from the Emperor relieving you of your command and instructing you to return to Rome. That would have been the end of your career, perhaps your freedom and possibly your life. Jesus would have been crucified eventually anyway. So what could you have gained?

The answer is that you would have gained *a great friendship*. That would have meant something to you, inasmuch as you probably didn't have a friend in the whole world. That doesn't make you unusual. Nothing is so rare as true friendship. Many a man, especially as he gets older, would gladly exchange all his wealth, power and prestige for one good friend who loves and appreciates him for himself. Jesus was that kind of friend to his disciples, and that's what he has proved himself to be again and again to the people who accept him and stand with him. He doesn't give them silver or gold or success or reputation but he does give them friendship, a lasting, dependable, unbreakable friendship that follows them to the ends of the earth and never lets them down. There was a missionary in the Pacific Islands whose young wife died and who had to dig her grave with his own hands, surrounded by savage and hostile faces. He later said, "I should have gone mad and died beside that lonely grave if it had not been for Christ and the friendship he vouchsafed to me there."

If you had been Pontius Pilate and had taken your stand with Jesus you would have gained *a great development*. Think of your evolution of character if you had lived for any length of time in the transforming company of Jesus. What a different person you would have become! Christ would have released you from fear and insecurity and set you free to be yourself. He would have brought you to your full potential as a human being. Few people achieve that. Few grow in all aspects of their personalities. Sometimes you do meet a whole person whose moral and spiritual development have kept pace with his growth in body and mind. Christ in his life on this earth was such a person. Surely you recognised that, as others recognised it and begged him to share his life with them. Christ does that for people who take a stand with him. He would have done the same for you.

If you had been Pontius Pilate and had taken your stand with Jesus you would have gained *a great purpose*. There can be no greater purpose than that of the early Christians committed to penetrating a pagan world with the redeeming Gospel of God's love. Think of Paul pursuing his perilous missionary journeys over land and sea and contrast him with yourself in your retirement luxuriating in the Roman baths to heal the hangover of the night before. There were two realities in your world — a dying Empire that looked to the past and a newborn Religion that looked to the future. There are two realities in our world — a sick civilisation that will surely die and a company of the committed that contains the seeds of new life. To that company belong the men and women of our generation who take their stand with Jesus.

CHAPTER NOTES:

1. Reported in *The Globe and Mail,* Toronto, October 8, 1974
2. John 19:11
3. John 18:28-31
4. Luke 23:2
5. john 18:33-38
6. Luke 23:5
7. Luke 23:6-12
8. Matt. 27:15-23
9. John 19-1-7
10. John 19:8-12
11. Matt. 27:24-26
12. John 19:19-22
13. Matt. 27:57-61
14. Matt. 27:62-66

16
Herod Antipas

"That Fox"

SOME PEOPLE ARE so like animals in their behaviour, habits
and character that they give real credence to the theory of
evolution. There are many different types in the human zoo,
some lovable, others not so lovable. If you call a man a lion you
probably admire his greath strength. If you call a child a little
monkey you are telling him with affection that he is mischie-
vous and elusive. Call someone a dog or a pig or a snake or a
toad or a wolf and you are not being so complimentary. Call
him a fox and you probably don't trust him; you consider him
the tricky type, cunning, clever and cowardly.

That's what Jesus called Herod Antipas, the Tetrarch of
Galilee. He was the only character in the Gospel drama to
whom Jesus ever referred by the name of an animal. He spoke
lovingly of his sheep and lambs in the collective sense but for
Herod alone he showed the measure of his contempt by
comparing him to a beast of prey. On his way to Jerusalem
some of the Pharisees came to him and said, "You should
leave this place and go your way; Herod is out to kill you."
Jesus replied, "Go and tell that fox, 'Listen: today and
tomorrow I shall be casting out devils and working cures; on
the third day I reach my goal'.[1] Jesus was not afraid of Herod
Antipas. He knew that the little puppet king did not have the
guts to kill him. The man was more like a fox than a wolf. He
might terrorise the barnyard fowl; but when it came to bigger
game, he had to get others to do his dirty work for him.

His father, King Herod the Great, did try to kill Jesus
when he was a baby in his mother's arms.[2] As we saw in an

earlier chapter, God finished that story. The younger Herod succeeded his father, though not to the whole Jewish kingdom as he had originally expected. Ultimately he received only the northern provinces of Galilee and Perea which he seems to have governed with moderate success. Like his father he was distinguished for his love of building. Among other things he built as his capital a new city on the western shore of the Sea of Galilee which he called Tiberius in honour of the Emperor and which remains as the only populated city on the Sea of Galilee today.

Antipas seems to have inherited all that was worst in his father's character. The older Herod, in spite of his violent intrigues and murderous schemes, did have a few manly qualities. After all, history does remember him as Herod the Great. By no possibility could his second son ever have become a great man. Historians and biographers agree that he was a weak, cruel, sensuous, ostentatious, shallow-hearted creature whose tragic exploits are plainly written for everyone to read. He married the daughter of Aretas, king of the Nabataeans. Then he went to Rome where he visited the house of his half-brother, Herod Philip. This Herod had married Herodias, his niece, and by her had a daughter, Salome. Antipas fell violently in love with Herodias, his half-sister-in-law by marriage, and determined to divorce his wife and marry her. The daughter of Aretas fled to her father for protection.

Two of the more authentic characters in the rock opera, *Jesus Christ Superstar*,[3] are Judas Iscariot and Herod Antipas. With others the authors have allowed their imagination to take liberties, but Judas and Herod appear exactly as we picture them after reading the Gospels. Herod in his single scene comes across as a gluttonous, dissipated, sulky, petulant, superficial creature who is less than a man. You see him in the motion picture version surrounded by his harem and showing a vast expanse of bare, bloated belly. You hear him singing his rag-time song with the unforgettable line, "Walk across my swimming pool".

"Walk Across My Swimming Pool"

Herod makes his first appearance in the Gospel drama at

the execution of John the Baptist. There is reason to suppose
that he respected John and perhaps even feared him a little.
At any rate, he wanted this good and holy man to approve of
his divorce and incestuous remarriage, just as Henry VIII
wanted Sir Thomas More to approve of his marital adven-
tures. In both cases the man of God said No and was
imprisoned and lost his head. To guard John against the fury
of his vengeful wife Herod placed him in protective custody
in the fortress of Machaerus. There he visited him from time
to time and made up a congregation of one while John
preached. John didn't convert Herod but he did get through
to him and start him thinking. Then came the famous
birthday party when Salome danced, and Herod, presumably
half-drunk, promised her any reward, and her mother
prompted her to demand the head of John the Baptist on a
meat platter. That greatly distressed Herod who was not
anxious to have the blood of a prophet on his hands, but the
circumstances gave him no choice, and he reluctantly ordered
John's execution.[4]

The Gospels play that story as a kind of flash-back, an
interlude wedged between two scenes in the narrative.[5]
Having trained his disciples to share his ministry of teaching
and healing, Jesus sends them out in pairs to do it on their
own. They perform such miracles and attract such notice that
Herod hears about it and starts worrying all over again.
People are saying about Jesus that he is John the Baptist
come back to life, and that's what Herod is afraid of. He says,
"This is John, whom I beheaded, raised from the dead."
There is truth as well as superstition in that fear. Herod could
murder John but he could not murder the God who spoke
through John. That God was now getting at him in another
way. Luke's Gospel places a different construction on Herod's
reaction to Jesus. He doesn't believe the rumours and he is
not afraid, only curious. He says, " 'As for John, I beheaded
him myself; but who is this that I hear such talk about?' And
he was anxious to see him."[6]

Herod got his wish handed to him on a silver platter. It
occurred on the Friday morning of Passover Week when he
happened to be in Jerusalem for the celebration of the
festival. Suddenly a shouting crowd approached his palace.

They came from the house of Pontius Pilate, the Roman
Governor of Judea, bringing with them a prisoner who had
been on trial for his life. The prisoner was none other than
Jesus of Nazareth. One of the priests may have handed a note
to Herod which read, in effect, "Most illustrious Prince
Herod, the prisoner is a Galilean and comes under your
jurisdiction. Not wishing to usurp your prerogatives, I am
remitting the case to you. Respectfully, Pontius Pilate." That
didn't fool Herod. He himself was an expert in passing the
buck and he was not about to dirty his hands with the blood
of a second prophet. However, he was pleased to see Jesus, he
had wanted to see him for a long time, he had heard that the
man could perform miracles. Perhaps he could be persuaded
to perform one right now. That would be entertaining.[7]

You can picture the scene which must have been on a
grander and more dramatic scale than that suggested by
Superstar. The stage is set like a royal courtroom, with marble
floors and velvet tapestries and sniggering courtiers prostrat-
ing themselves in stupid servility before their king. On the
throne sits Herod, the spineless worldling, gross, sensuous,
lustful and dissipated, his beady, foxy eyes peering out of his
puffy flesh. Jesus stands before him pale and exhausted but
perfectly poised, his manliness exaggerating the unmanliness
of the king. Herod stares at him insolently and cackles, "Well,
well, well! So you are the celebrated Jesus of Nazareth. We
are honoured. They tell us you perform miracles. Prove it to
us. Perform a miracle now. Break those chains on your wrists.
Turn this cup of water into wine. Walk across my swimming
pool." The courtiers giggle. Jesus says nothing. Herod tries to
break his silence by mocking him and ordering his soldiers to
laugh derisively. "This fellow pretends to be king of the Jews.
He doesn't look like a king. Let's make him look like a king.
Put a gorgeous robe on him... Hail, King of the Jews!" Still
not a word from Jesus. After a while Herod gets bored. "Oh
well, take him back to Pilate — with my thanks. He was good
for a few laughs anyway."

Trifling with God

Exit Herod from the stage of the Passion drama. In many

ways he comes across as the most despicable character in the cast. He didn't commit a major crime. If we put him in the dock along with the other defendants in the war crimes trial we have to find him innocent, even though he smells of guilt. He didn't condemn Jesus or sentence him or betray him or crucify him or join the jeering mob at the Cross. He simply refused to treat Jesus seriously. He wouldn't try the case, even though it came under his jurisdiction, and find the prisoner innocent, which he might have done without fear of Caiaphas and the priestly hierarchy. He was guilty not of commission but of omission. He came to the moment of truth, the most crucial encounter in his life, he stood face to face with the Incarnate Son of God and trifled with him. That was Herod's sin. And Jesus answered him nothing.

So it happens to all men who trifle with God's Christ, and there are such men even today, especially today. They are not the declared enemies of Christianity because they don't take it that seriously. They don't try to kill Jesus, they trifle with him. One of them was Bertrand Russell who wrote a provocative book entitled *Why I Am Not a Christian*[8] which, if read with an open mind, could have an effect exactly opposite from what Russell intended. He tries to put down Jesus, first by denying that he ever existed, then by showing that the Christ of the Gospels was really not a very wise or good man (p. 11). He concedes that religion has made some contributions to civilisation, such as helping to fix the calendar and chronicle eclipses of the sun, and adds, "These two services I am prepared to acknowledge but I do not know of any others" (p. 18). Russell knows very well that nothing can more effectively damn religion or any other enterprise than the focussing on its fringe features. He represents a whole secular culture, a world of art and journalism and theatre and television, that stands face to face with the Incarnate Son of God and trifles with him. And Christ makes no reply.

Much popular religion today is a trifling with Jesus, and that's why we can't get too enthusiastic over it. John summed up the purpose of the four Gospels and of the whole New Testament when he wrote, "These are written that you may believe that Jesus is the Christ, the Son of God, and that

believing you may have life in his name."[9] But the popular
Jesus, the Jesus of rock operas, youth movements and bumper
stickers, is not usually the Son of God. He is not Divine at all.
He is a folk-hero who fought against the establishment and
was martyred for it. He is the mascot of radicals, rebels and
do-gooders who are working off their resentments against
society. He is the man for others who ended up as a masochist
or a clown. Many so-called religious people, some of the most
religious people stand face to face, as Herod did, with the
Incarnate Son of God and trifle with him. Christ answers
them nothing.

Religious dilletantism is a trifling with God. We saw that
one of the ploys tried by the Samaritan woman to divert
attention from her adulterous life was to engage Jesus in a
discussion of where and how to worship God.[10] He refused to
be diverted. He said, in effect, "The place and techniques of
worship do not matter. What does matter is the sincerity of
your worship, the reality of your communion with God. True
worship is spiritual. You offer God not your words and your
praises but your life." Yet there are still people who try to
avoid a confrontation with God by focussing on worship and
other externals of religion. In fact, worship becomes a kind of
hobby with them. They become addicted to worship as others
are addicted to horse-racing and threatre-going and health
clubs and outdoor sports. They become church-hoppers,
sermon-tasters, connoisseurs of music and liturgy and archi-
tecture. Every Sunday they stand face to face with the
Incarnate Son of God and every Sunday they trifle with him.
Christ answers them nothing.

Christian morality can be a trifling with God. Blatty's
novel, *The Exorcist*,[11] focuses on the incarnation of evil in a
twelve-year-old girl, resulting in her blasphemous language
and obscene behaviour. The incident takes place in Washington just a short distance from the Pentagon where the
military establishment is planning the saturation bombing of
Cambodia. There is something symbolic about that juxtapo-
sition. Where does the greater concentration of evil lie? Not to
minimise the plight of the poor child, Christian morality
trivialises God by reducing him to the role of a Peeping Tom
who monitors all our naughty behaviour. I am sure that

many of the personal evils that used to trouble the Churches do not trouble God nearly as much as the Church's indifference to and involvement in the great social evils that stigmatize people, discriminate against them, exploit them, violate them and hold them down to a miserably low level of life.

Even prayer can be a trifling with God. When the World Council of Churches met at Evanston in 1954, the Religious Research Foundation drew our attention to a display in the lobby of the Georgian Hotel. In a glass case were two pie plates filled with earth, the first one sprouting a tiny garden, and the second one barren. Seeds had been planted in both plates, and each had been carefully watered and exposed to sunlight; but some pious people had prayed that one set of seeds would germinate and the other die. Their "experiment" having succeeded, they were saying in effect that if prayer can be seen to work in little things like the pair of pie plates, how can we doubt its power in the great issues of life? The point is that we do not doubt the power of prayer in the great issues of life. We do doubt whether we have the right to trifle with God and put prayer on the level of "Walk across my swimming pool".

The Silence of God

God will not be trifled with. He will be loved and adored and worshipped and feared and hated and cursed but he will not be trivialized. If men refuse to treat him seriously, if they try to trifle with him, he withdraws himself and keeps silent just as Jesus kept silent before Herod Antipas who thought that he could order up a work of God for his own amusement. That could go far toward explaining the mystery of unanswered prayer. It could explain the conspiracy against God, the cynicism, skepticism, agnosticism and outright atheism of much of our secular culture today. It was Paul Tillich who suggested that God may actually reveal himself by creating a silence about himself.[12] In order to protect the sanctity of his Name he may withhold from a generation what was natural to previous generations — the use of the word "God". When God hears his Name irreverently mouthed by people who have no serious intention of honouring it he may indeed create a silence about himself and withdraw his Name from currency until people learn again to speak that Name with reverence and godly fear.

So ends the story of Herod Antipas who was face to face with the Incarnate Son of God and refused to treat him seriously. He leaves the stage of the Passion drama like a man going into a great darkness. There are conflicting reports of what happened to him after that. Secular historians say that he was dreadfully defeated in battle against his first wife's father, Aretas, that he fell from his throne and was banished from his kingdom. The Book of Acts says that he persecuted the early Church, murdered at least one of the apostles, became drunk with illusions of his own divinity, suffered a fatal seizure and was "eaten up with worms and died".[13] Either way he suffered the fate of every man who tries to trifle with God's Christ. For a while God does not answer him, then he gives him a terrible answer, not in words but in events. It is all the more tragic because it might have ended so differently. If Herod had taken the case on Good Friday, treated Jesus seriously, given him a fair triall, proclaimed his innocence as the pentitent thief proclaimed it from the Cross, Jesus might have given Herod the promise that he gave to the penitent thief, a promise that avails for all eternity: *"Today you shall be with me in Paradise."*[14]

CHAPTER NOTES:

1.	Luke 13:31-32	9.	John 21:31 (R.S.V.)
2.	Matt. 2:16-18	10.	John 4:19-24
3.	Op cit.	11.	Op cit.
4.	Mark 6:17-29	12.	Paul Tillich, *The Eternal*
	Mark 6:7-14		*Now* (S.C.M. Press,
6.	Luke 9:7-9		London, 1963) p. 84
7.	Luke 23:6-12	13.	Acts 12:20-23
8.	London, George Allen	14.	Luke 23:39-43
	and Unwin Ltd., 1957		

V

These Watched Him Die

17
The Centurion

The Guilt

HAVE YOU EVER been given a routine job to do that turned out to be one of the most difficult and distasteful things that you have ever done in your life? Have you ever taken part in a proceeding that was completely within the law but that left you with a nagging sense of guilt? Have you ever helped to bring a criminal to justice and come away with the feeling that you were the real criminal? Have you ever committed an act of violence that will haunt you for the rest of your days, a destructive deed for which you can never forgive yourself? If so, you will understand the story that I am going to tell you now.

I am a centurion in the army of Tiberius Caesar, Emperor of Rome and supreme governor of the world. Better that I should remain nameless, though tradition calls me Longinus. I have never told my story to anyone before, not even to my wife. I couldn't bring myself to tell her, though by all the gods she deserved some explanation of my strange moods and behaviour when I came home on retirement leave. I wasn't able to sleep, I couldn't eat my meals, I sat silent for hours, I refused to see our friends. Sometimes I left the house in the middle of the night and walked the city streets until dawn. She must have found me intolerable to live with. She must have suspected that I were ill or had another woman. If only it had been that simple!

How could I tell her that I had crucified an innocent man? Not only innocent — that happens sometimes — but the best and bravest man I have ever met anywhere in the world. The image of him hanging on his cross will haunt me to the end of time. I can argue that I was only obeying orders and that if I had not done the deed others would have done it, but that doesn't soften the pain of my guilt. I executed him. I commanded the detail that put him to death. If history ever brought to trial all the characters responsible for the crucifixion of that innocent man, I should not only be found guilty but I should plead guilty.

Please understand that I am not a squeamish person. Otherwise I should never have become a soldier, never have been made a centurion. Let me explain that a centurion was not a commissioned officer like a tribune; he didn't have the social standing or the political pull to qualify for that. He was more like a sergeant who rose from the ranks to command a hundred men in recognition of his bravery and qualities of leadership. I received my promotion while fighting against the army of Germanicus in Dalmatia. I was already looking forward to retirement when I was transferred against my wish to a Syrian legion with headquarters at Caesarea. I say "against my wish", because the Jews were reputed to be a troublesome people, as Pontius Pilate quickly discovered when he became Governor of Judea and Jerusalem.

Yet I did not find them troublesome. On the contrary, I found them fascinating, as did many of my comrades. Some people think that all professional soldiers, as a result of fighting battles and living in barracks, are hard, cruel, tough and insensitive to the finer things of life. That's not true. Soldiers are people with the same feelings as other people. They can be sensitive and sympathetic; and, perhaps as a result of keeping close company with death, they can be profoundly religious men. That's what attracted us to the Jews. They are profoundly religious people, and their religion is not so confusing as ours. Some of our soldiers responded positively to the preaching of John the Baptist.[1] Others were actually converted to Judaism. One of my fellow-centurions provided the money to build a synagogue in Capernaum and earned the highest possible praise for his religious faith.[2] Of course, that's only a small part of the picture.

The Scourging

Most Jews hated their Roman oppressors and wanted to drive us into the sea. Certain elements in Jewish society were always plotting rebellion. They usually surfaced during Passover Week, the great Jewish festival which recalled the release of their ancestors from slavery and their crossing of the Red Sea to freedom. During that week we were transferred from Caesarea to Jerusalem to strengthen the garrison there just in case the Jews decided to try a repeat performance of the exodus from Egypt. On Friday morning I was resting in the barracks and feeling fortunate that things had gone so smoothly, when suddenly an order came from the Governor to prepare an execution detail. That meant myself and four soldiers. I groaned. An execution could take all day, perhaps several days. Whoever the victim was, I would be responsible from the moment he was delivered into my hand until I turned him over to those who claimed his lifeless body. I never liked executions, but they had to be carried out and they were pretty much routine. In this case I couldn't understand why the Governor wanted the whole company present.

We paraded before the barracks, I inspected the men, and we marched over to the Governor's palace. A trial had taken place, the prisoner had been sentenced, but I couldn't see him very well. Poor devil! What had he done to deserve the death sentence. There were two others standing near him, and I could tell right away what they had done to deserve the death sentence. They were criminals and they looked the part.

Then came the order that always made me ashamed of being a Roman: "Scourge the prisoner." We don't just execute our criminals, we torture them first. Luckily for some of them they don't survive the torture. I'll spare you a description of it. Enough to say that we tied the victim to a post and lashed him with whips until his flesh hung in ribbons and he was drenched with his own blood. I had seen scores of men scourged but I never could become hardened to it. Some whimpered and pleaded for mercy, some burst their bonds and flung themselves on the scourger, some contorted like a nest of smitten vipers. This man wasn't like any of them. He didn't cringe or boast, he didn't wince or yield, he didn't curse or cry.

I turned to one of my men and asked, "Who is the prisoner? What's his name?" He replied, "Jesus of Nazareth." I asked, "What is the charge against him?" The answer came back, "He calls himself the king of the Jews." The name spread like a sick joke throughout the whole company. Someone began to laugh, then others joined him until the pavement beneath our feet echoed with a chorus of mocking laughter. "King of the Jews! Let's make him a king then!"

They pushed him on a low chair, threw a purple robe over his bleeding back and put a stick in his hand. Someone made a crown of thorny twigs and stuck it at a crazy angle on his head. Then they all began bowing and scraping before him as though he were the Emperor, crying out in derision, "Hail, King of the Jews!"[3] One beaten, broken, defenceless man against a whole company of soldiers. Some odds! At length I could stand it no longer. "Enough of this!" I shouted. "Bring his cross!"

The Cross

My friends, have you ever seen pictures of a Roman cross? It was massively built. The upright beam, which measured about nine feet, remained permanently at the place of execution. The cross beam, which usually measured seven or eight feet, was carried there by the victim in a procession. It was not all that heavy, unless he had just been scourged. He also carried a piece of wood covered with white gypsum on which the nature of his offence was written in black letters. It all served as an object lesson to any other potential criminals who happened to be lurking about the city streets that day. We closed our ranks and started the slow procession to Golgotha.

The street was lined with spectators, ten-deep, all craning their necks to see the sordid show. Some were jeering, others weeping, most of them silent. I could read the hatred in their eyes. Suddenly Jesus stumbled under the weight of the cross. He couldn't carry it an inch further. I looked around and saw a broad-shouldered black man in the front of the line. "You," I shouted, "get in here and carry it for him."[4] He seemed about to refuse, but I drew my sword, and that quickly changed his mind. Then I threw some water on the prisoner's face. For the first time I saw his face. It was caked with blood and masked in pain, but there was no hatred in his eyes. The procession moved on. Jesus whispered something to the black man, but I couldn't hear what he said. I did hear him say to some sobbing women, "Do not weep for me."[5] I thought, "You had better weep for him. Someone had better weep for him."

We got to Golgotha, the skull-shaped hill outside the city wall, poetically chosen for crucifixions. The crowds surged after us. I could see that it was going to be quite a show. Now came the part that I hated most — the nailing of the victims to their crosses. That was where most prisoners went berserk. I have seen them shrieking in agony, whining for mercy, struggling madly with the soldiers, fighting like crazed animals. It often took half a dozen men to hold a prisoner to his cross while we fastened him there. We always did one merciful thing. We offered the victim a draught of drugged wine to deaden his pain. The other two criminals gulped theirs eagerly. But not Jesus. He refused it. He evidently wanted to die with a clear head. He stretched out on his cross as though he wanted it, needed it. My men drove a spike through his right hand, another through his left hand. They flattened the soles of his feet against the upright beam and drove another great spike through both of them. His blood spurted all over the place. The sound of his crunching bones sickened me, but there was no sound from him, no resistance, no struggle.

That's when I began to realise that this was no ordinary crucifixion. I am a soldier. All my life I have dealt in blood and pain and death. I have seen men die in many different circumstances and I recognise courage when I see it; but never have I seen anything like this man's calmness and courage and perfect poise in the face of death. This was something utterly new and strange in all my professional experience. For the first time I began to wonder if there had been a mistake, a dreadful miscarriage of justice. Was this man really innocent of the crime laid against him? Had he been framed? Little did I know how many illegalities it took to put him on that cross.

"Jesus of Nazareth, King of the Jews."[6] Pontius Pilate wrote that inscription in three languages on the wood that we nailed to the head of the cross. That piece of irony completed, my men hoisted the huge cross and dropped it into its socket with a loud thud that must have jarred his body with unspeakable pain. His blood trickled down the side of the cross, staining it forever. Flies buzzed around his mouth and settled on his wounds. My soldiers had removed his only item of clothing, a seamless tunic of rather fine quality. They began fighting over it, then they decided to gamble for it.[7] I didn't stop them. They had to do something to fill in the long hours.

The Crucified

The crowd closed in and began making fun of him: " 'Ah!'

they cried, wagging their heads, 'You would pull the temple down, would you, and build it in three days? Come down from the cross and save yourself!' " The priests had an answer for that one as they joked with one another. " 'He saved others', they said, 'but he cannot save himself. Let the Messiah, the king of Israel, come down now from the cross. If we see that, we shall believe!' "[8] He made no reply, just hung there and took their mockery. When my soldiers joined in the jeering I saw his lips moving, but he wasn't looking at us. He was looking at the sky and he seemed to be praying. Above the noise I could hear him say, "Father, forgive them; they do not know what they are doing."[9] That sent my men into gales of laughter. They knew what they were doing right enough. I wasn't so sure.

Another voice rose above the roar of the crowd, a harsh, taunting voice: "Are you the Messiah? Save yourself and us." We had crucified the two criminals one on either side of Jesus, and here was one of them spitting for the last time at fate by cursing the poor defenceless wretch between them. He had scarcely closed his mouth when his companion in crime cried out at him from the other cross, "Have you no fear of God? You are under the same sentence as he is. For us it is plain justice; we are paying the price for our misdeeds; but this man has done nothing wrong." "Nothing wrong?" I said to myself, "What a pity Pontius Pilate didn't see it that way — or maybe he did." Jesus turned and looked at him, and there was gratitude in his eyes, and recognition as though they had met somewhere before. They looked at each other for a long time as though they were the only two men in the world. Suddenly the thief said, "Jesus" — I heard no one else call him by that familiar name — "remember me when you come to your throne". Throne! Is that what he calls a grave? Jesus answered him, "I tell you this: today you shall be with me in Paradise".[10]

I can't describe to you what happened in my mind at that moment. Suddenly I realized that everything was crazy, and the whole world was upside down. It was like a Greek tragedy where all the characters, the heroes and villains, had got their roles reversed. We had nailed this man to the cross, yet he seemed to control the situation. He, the victim of this mad débâcle, was the one person unshaken by it. We were putting him to death, but he seemed to be laying down his life of his own accord. Who

THESE WATCHED HIM DIE

were the real criminals that day? Had we judged him, or was he judging us? Had we broken him, or was he breaking us?

There were a few people at the cross who did not join in the general uproar. They stood in a little group by themselves, huddled together in grief and fear and shame. I noticed a middle-aged woman at the centre of them and decided from the way she looked at Jesus that she must be his mother. I remembered my own mother and tried to avert this woman's eyes. Suddenly he looked directly at her and at the young man holding her arm and said through his pain, "Mother, there is your son"; and to the young man, "There is your mother".[11] I don't think he wanted them to be there at the end. With a last sorrowful look at the cross, they went away. Yet I knew that they would be back.

When Jesus spoke again, it was with a sound like that of a croaking animal — "I thirst."[12] No wonder! We all felt thirsty. The noonday sun had climbed high in the sky, scorching the whole earth beneath our feet. I dipped a sponge in a jar of sour wine, stuck it on the tip of a javelin and held it to his parched lips. He sipped it gratefully. He could be grateful to the man who crucified him.

The Darkness

Then it got dark. That noonday sun went out of the sky, and darkness covered Calvary like a blanket, a dense darkness that lasted for three hours. It silenced everybody — the priests and the spectators and my soldiers and the men dying on their crosses. Time stood still in that dark silence, and I wondered if it was nature's way of covering up a dreadful, despicable deed. Then a cry pierced the silence, a chilling, unearthly cry from the centre cross that must have carried to the end of the world: "My God, my God, why hast thou forsaken me?"[13] I don't know who his god was, but he certainly answered him in the crashing thunder and streaks of lightning and drenching rain. I found myself wishing that his god would rescue him from the cursed cross forever.

But it was too late for that. Through the darkness came another piercing cry, "It is finished." I thanked whatever gods there might be that it was all over for him, yet that wasn't exactly what he said. He said, "It is accomplished,"[14] as though by dying there upon the cross he had finished something tremendously important that had been given him to do. Again I had the strange feeling that he really controlled the events of that dreadful day. This thing wasn't just happening to him; he was doing it. He died as a creative deed. "Father," he shouted, and it was a shout of triumph, "into thy hands I commit my spirit." [15]

Then all hell broke loose. The earth trembled beneath our feet; great, gaping fissures appeared in front of us; I could hear the noise of rocks splitting and buildings falling.[16] The people went crazy with fear. This thing hadn't turned out as they expected at all. They ran away like a stampede of frightened animals, beating their breasts and screaming at the top of their voices.[17] Soon Calvary was deserted, except for my small squad of soldiers left to guard the lonely corpses on that skull-shaped hill.

For a long time I stood there looking at Jesus. I didn't know anything else about him but I was sure of one thing. The penitent thief had said it: "This man has done nothing wrong." I had executed an innocent man and I confessed it aloud to my soldiers: "Beyond all doubt this man was innocent."[18] Yet it wasn't his innocence alone that overpowered me in that moment and will haunt me for the rest of my life. It was an awareness, that I shall never be able to shake off, that this innocent man, who died like a soldier and was mourned by the elements, was more than a man. Falling to my knees, I said something then that I shall keep on saying through all eternity and that I want to say to you right now: *"Truly this man was a son of God."*[19]

CHAPTER NOTES

1. Luke 3:14
2. Lukee 7:1-10
3. Mark 15:16-20
4. Luke 23:26
5. Luke 23:27-31
6. John 19:19-22
7. John 19:23-24
8. Mark 15:29-32
9. Luke 23:34
10. Luke 23:29-43
11. John 19:25-27
12. John 19:28-29
13. Matt. 27:46
14. John 19:30
15. Luke 23:46
16. Matt. 27:50-52
17. Luke 23:48
18. Luke 23:47
19. Mark 15:39

18
Barabbas

A Good Friday for Him

IN EVERY HUMAN tragedy one character seems to come out on
top. Not only so, but he actually benefits from the misery and
suffering of all the other characters around him. The irony of
it is that very often he is the person who least deserves it.
That's what happened on Good Friday. There was one man
for whom it was really a *good* Friday. For nearly everyone else
it turned out to be a bad, black and horrible day — for Jesus
who died on the Cross, for the two thieves who were crucified
with him, for Judas who committed suicide, for the disciples
who lost their dearest friend, Pilate who lost his self-respect,
the soldiers who crucified an innocent man, the crowds who
ran home beating their breasts. Only one man rose above the
whole débâcle and emerged not only unscathed but in better
circumstances that he ever dared to dream. That man was
Barabbas who gained his freedom at the expense of Jesus.

There is no way that we can do a character study of
Barabbas. His character, his personality do not emerge. He
does nothing and says nothing, i.e., nothing which has been
recorded in any of the four Gospels, though he appears briefly
in all of them. The French playwright, Ghelderode, shows
him in the dungeon waiting to be executed. He is a tough,
unrepentant ruffian who boasts of his murderous exploits and
declares proudly that it took a whole battalion of soldiers to
arrest him and bring him to justice. A priest comes to the
door of the dungeon and whispers that things may not turn
out as badly as he expects. Next we see him on Pilate's
balcony where Caiaphas eloquently presents him to the

crowd as a basically patriotic man who is more sinned against than sinning and who deserves a better chance in life. He keeps prodding Barabbas to shed a few tears and put on a show of contrition, even though it means nothing. When the crowd votes for his freedom, he sheds a few more tears and promises to be a good citizen. When he sees Jesus being led to the gallows prepared for him he realises that he has been cleverly used. Running towards Jesus, he calls, "Hey, comrade! It's not my fault... No ill feeling?"[1]

To return to the facts, however, Barabbas in the Gospel drama is entirely passive. We don't know a thing that he did on Good Friday, only what happened to him. What did happen was so tremendous that, in spite of himself, he stands out as one of the most important characters in the Crucifixion event and in all sacred history. Barabbas has the unique distinction of being the first man who could say with literal truth, "Jesus died for me". That has become the central theme of all Christian devotion, it has been said by countless people through the centuries, but Barabbas was the first person who could say it and mean it. He was the great beneficiary of the Good Friday tragedy, the man who, though he least deserved it, came out on top. In that sense he is a representative character — a truth which becomes increasingly plain as we put together all the facts that we know about him.

A Representative Character

The first fact that we know about Barabbas is that he should have been on the cross. That comes across loud and clear from the Gospel record. He is variously listed as a man of some notoriety, a bandit, a rebel, an insurrectionist and a murderer.[2] He was in prison because he deserved to be there. He was doomed to die, because death was the prescribed penalty for the crimes which he had committed against society. If Pilate, under normal circumstances, had sentenced him to death, there would not have been a murmur or criticism. If he had been crucified along with the other criminals, not a tear would have been shed. Barabbas should have been on the cross.

In that sense Barabbas represents all criminals who deserve

to be punished for their crimes. He is the mugger who smashes the jaw of an old lady and snatches the few dollars from her purse; the rapist who drags an innocent child into a dark alley and violates her body and soul; the thief who steals company funds to pay his gambling debts and throws his partners into bankruptcy; the loan shark who gets helpless people in his clutches and keeps them poor for the rest of their lives; the agitator who incites gullible young people to destroy public property; the hijacker who terrorises the passengers on an aeroplane; the kidnapper who bargains the life of his victim for an exorbitant ransom; the murderer who coolly and calculatingly puts a bullet in a human heart. The prisons are full of men like Barabbas; and if the police had their way, they would remain longer in prison and be joined by many others. The guardians of law and order feel frustrated by the travesty of justice that so often lets Barabbas off with a light sentence, then paroles him to continue being a menace to society. They believe that there is too much sympathy for Barabbas and not enough for his victims.

In a larger sense Barabbas represents all people who have broken the moral laws of God and who therefore stand guilty before the bar of God's justice. "Thou shalt have no other gods before me."[3] Barabbas is every man who keeps God very low in his list of priorities. "Thou shalt not make unto thee any graven image"; Barabbas is every man who tries to cut God down to his own size. "Thou shalt not take the name of the Lord thy God in vain"; Barabbas is every man who speaks the name of God without sincerity. "Remember the sabbath day to keep it holy"; Barabbas is every man who desecrates all sacred institutions. "Honour thy father and thy mother"; Barabbas is every man who brings grief and dishonour to his parents. "Thou shalt not kill"; Barabbas is every man who destroys the life of another man. "Thou shalt not commit adultery"; Barabbas is every man who cannot remain faithful to his wife. "Thou shalt not steal"; Barabbas is every man who makes a dishonest income tax return. "Thou shalt not bear false witness"; Barabbas is every man who tells lies about another person. "Thou shalt not covet"; Barabbas is every man who desires what rightfully belongs to someone else. Barabbas represents all of us in his guilt before God. He should have been on the cross.

Amazing Grace

The second fact that we know about Barabbas is that he did nothing to earn his pardon. To our knowledge he made no appeal for clemency, no promise of atonement, no guarantee of good behaviour in the future. He did not send a message to Pontius Pilate or plead with the priests to intercede for him. Having been arrested and imprisoned and sentenced to death for his crimes against society, he presumably accepted his fate. He was prepared to die, he expected to die, he deserved to die. Barabbas played no part in the events that impinged on his life and resulted in his undreamed-of pardon. The factors that saved him and set him free worked entirely outside himself.

Look at some of those fortuitous factors. Barabbas happened to be in prison on the Friday of Passover Week, the one week in the year when the Roman Governor granted the gift of clemency to a Jewish prisoner. His full name happened to be Jesus bar Abbas; and it happened that on that very day another Jesus, named Jesus of Nazareth, was on trial for his life. It happened also that the priests particularly wanted Jesus of Nazareth to die. The judge happened to be Pontius Pilate who did not have the courage to defy the priests and acquit an innocent man. Looking for a loophole, Pilate happened to hit on the idea of presenting his annual Passover gift in the form of a choice, making the mob choose freedom for one of the two men named Jesus. At that moment a message happened to come from his wife, diverting his attention long enough to allow the priests to circulate among the people and plump for Barabbas. The mob, that happened to be a typical victim of mob psychology, chose Barabbas, and Pilate had to set him free. He was probably the most surprised man in the world. On any other day and under any other circumstances he would have been taken from the dungeon and marched in a procession to Golgotha, carrying his cross, and there he would have been crucified. That was the appointed schedule of events, and there was nothing he could do to alter it. He was saved and set free only because Jesus of Nazareth entered the picture and touched his life.

In that sense Barabbas represents and illustrates the whole Christian Gospel. The Gospel is the good news of something which God has done for our salvation, something entirely outside ourselves which we do not deserve and cannot earn. The Appostle Paul made that the central theme of his theology, because it was the central discovery and experience of his life. He wrote of it in his letters: "For by grace you have been saved through faith; and this is not your own doing, it is the gift of God."[4] Martin Luther made the same discovery. To work out his salvation he ran the gamut of the whole Roman Catholic penitential system but with a sense of futility that made him physically ill and brought him to the brink of death. At last it dawned on him, as he read the letters of Paul, that man does not earn his salvation; he receives it from God through faith in Jesus Christ. John Wesley made the same discovery, as he confessed after his profound spiritual experience at Aldersgate: "I felt I did trust in Christ, Christ alone for my salvation. And an assurance was given me that he had taken away my sins, even mine, and saved me from the law of sin and death."

Barabbas did not trust in Christ for his salvation. He had never heard of Christ. In that larger sense he represents all the children of God, all the inhabitants of the world, all the generations since time began, the people of all races, religions, cultures and civilisations whom God in Christ reconciled to himself on Calvary's Cross. Roger Pilkington in one of his books tells that he was talking with the Dean of a cathedral about the rumour that a flying saucer full of scaly little men had landed somewhere on our planet. The Dean said, "Do you realise that at any moment such a vehicle might land right here in the Deanery Yard? And if so," he added, "it would be my job as an ordained priest and minister of the Gospel to go out there and talk to the crew about Jesus Christ. I confess that I find myself singularly ill-equipped for the task".[5] Ill-eequipped or not, the Dean had caught the New Testament view of the Cross as God's mighty act of salvation that includes all the creatures in his universe whether or not they have earned it or even heard of it.

A Ransom for Many

The third fact that we know about Barabbas is that Jesus died in his place. That was literally true. He was not unconditionally pardoned by the Roman Governor but given his pardon because a substitute had been found to take his place on the cross and pay the penalty that he should have paid. He owed his freedom to Jesus, not because Jesus somehow secured it for him but because Jesus took his place and died on the very cross that was probably intended for him.

We don't know whether Barabbas celebrated his unexpected and unearned reprieve by following the crowds to Calvary to see the sordid show. We don't know whether he joined the spectators who watched Jesus slowly dying under the noonday sun. If he did go to Calvary, and if he had a grain of feeling in his heart and an ounce of logic in his head, he must surely have said to himself, "That man is dying in my place. I should be up there on that cross. He is paying the penalty for my crimes."

That's what Christian theology has always called the substitutionary theory of the atonement. It is the oldest interpretation of what actually happened on the cross and it derives from the words of Jesus himself: "For even the Son of Man did not come to be served but to serve, and to surrender his life as a ransom for many."[6] Today we might call it the kidnapping theory, inasmuch as kidnapping has become the new political tool of extremists and terrorists. It is a despicable tool that requires no amount of courage but does require a total absence of human decency and sympathy. South American guerrillas abduct a foreign diplomat and announce that they will execute him unless his government pays $2 million and their government releases other guerrillas from prison. The ransom is always high, unreasonable and sometimes almost impossible. The Church of the Middle Ages believed that the Devil kidnapped the whole human race and demanded as a ransom the costliest and best that God could give — the life of his only-begotten Son. We celebrate the old-fashioned theory in our Good Friday hymns, "There was no other good enough to pay the price of sin..." Even our more sophisticated theologians still see a substitutionary element in the Cross. Emil Brunner expressed it powerfully and profoundly:

> In the Cross of Christ God says to man: There is where you ought to be. Jesus, my Son, hangs there in your stead. You are the rebel who should be hanged on the gallows. But lo, I suffer instead of you and because of you, because I love you in spite of what you are. My love for you is so great that I meet you there with my love, there on the Cross. I cannot meet you anywhere else. You must meet me there by identifying yourself with the One on the Cross. It is by this identification that I, God, can meet you, man, in him, saying to you what I say to him, "My beloved Son."[7]

The Constraint of the Cross

The fourth fact is a question — What happened to Barabbas after he gained his freedom at the expense of Jesus? Here the novelists and playwrights take over. In Ghelderode's play Barabbas gets drunk, goes to Calvary, sees the horrible injustice of it and vows vengeance on behalf of Jesus. He has no other choice because he has become an outcast, rejected by everyone, even his former friends who seem to say, "What are you doing walkinng about? Your place is on the cross". He chides the disciples for their cowardice and declares that he will act without them. Suddenly there is a clap of thunder and a loud cry from the Cross. In the ensuing riot someone comes behind Barabbas and thrusts a knife into his back. As he falls to the ground he reaches in the direction of Calvary and cries, "Hey! Jesus! I too am bleeding. Sacrificed the same day... But you died for something. I am dying for nothing. Nevertheless it's because of you...for you...Jesus..."[8]

The more familiar story, a novel by the Swedish author Par Lagerkvist,[9] was made into a motion picture. Again Barabbas gets drunk after his pardon and again goes to Golgotha and stares transfixed at the human scapegoat to whom he owes his life. He returns to his criminal ways and is soon caught and put back in the dungeon. This time he is not sentenced to death but condemned to a lifetime of hard labour in the copper mines of Cyprus. For twenty years he toils in that underground hell where most men die within a year. He not only lives but emerges with the strength and physique of a young man. He seems ageless. He is greatly influenced by Sahak, another slave who has become a Christian. They go to Rome where they become gladiators, fighting to the death before Caesar and the crowds in the Coliseum. Barabbas is not only ageless but invincible. He cannot die even if he wants to. To identify with what he believes the Christians are doing, he sets fire to a number of buildings in the city. At last we see him on a cross among endless rows of crosses, embracing that instrument of torture as though he needs and wants it more than anything else in the world and crying out in the darkness, "To thee I deliver my soul."

Either of those stories might have been true. It is impossible to believe that Barabbas could say "Jesus died for me" and be totally unaffected. That's what makes him a representative figure. No man with a grain of feeling in his heart or an ounce of logic in his head can ever be the same again once he has exposed himself to the Cross of Christ with any degree of understanding of what God has done for him there.

In his book, *Through the Valley of the Kwai*, Ernest Gordon, describing his experiences in a Japanese prisoner-of-war camp, tells that one of the most important factors that awakened religious faith in his fellow-prisoners was the Crucifixion. He says, "The crucifixion was seen as being of utmost relevance to our situation. A God who remained indifferent to the plight of his creatures was not a God with whom we could agree. The Crucifixion, however, told us that God was in our midst, suffering with us."[10] The Cross identifies God with man. It brings God all the way into our human experiences of failure, suffering, defeat and death. It shows that God loves us more than we can possibly imagine, that God will go to any length to demonstrate his love and that nothing can separate us from the love of God. Through the Cross of Christ God seems to say, "You can do with me what you like; you can break my bones and bruise my flesh and drain my blood, but you cannot stop me from being what I am, the Father who loves you and will not let you go".

There is a story, probably based on fact, about an Archbishop of Paris who was preaching to a great congregation. He told about three young men, gay, worldly and godless, who wandered into the cathedral one day. Two of them wagered the third that he would not make a bogus confession. He accepted the wager. The priest, who listened, realised what was happening, so when the pretending penitent had finished, he said, "To every confession there is a penance. You see the great Crucifix over there? Go to it, kneel down, and repeat three times as you look up into the face of the crucified, 'All this you did for me, and I don't care a damn!' " The young man emerged from the confessional box to report what had happened and to claim the wager from his companions. "Oh no," they said, "first complete the penance, then we will pay the wager." Walking slowly to the great Crucifix, he knelt down and looked up into that face with its searching eyes of aggrieved love. Then he began, "All this you did for me, and I..." He got not further. Tears flooded his eyes. His heart was torn by the pain of repentance. There his old life ended, and there the new began. Finishing his sermon, the Archbishop said, "I was that young man."

CHAPTER NOTES:

1. Michel de Ghelderode *Seven Plays*, Voolume 1 (Copyright 1960 by Hill and Wang Inc., New York) p.92
2. Mark 15:6-15; Matt. 27:15-23 Luke 23:18-19; John 18:39-40
3. Exodus 20:1-17 (K.J.V.)
4. Eph. 2:8 (R.S.V.)
5. Roger Pilkington, *World Without End* (Collins Fontana Books, London, 1961) p. 37
6. Mark 10:45
7. Emil Brunner, *Faith, Hope and Love* (Westminster Press, Philadelphia, 1956) p. 21
8. Op. cit. p. 123
9. Par Lagerkvist, *Barabbas* (Clark, Irwin and Company Ltd., Toronto; Chatto and Windus, London)
10. Ernest Gordon, *Through the Valley of the Kwai* (Harper and Row, New York and Evanston 1962) p. 139

19
Joseph of Arimathea

The Facts about Joseph

Is IT FAIR to judge any man on the basis of one qualifying phrase in his biography? That's what we seem to have done with Joseph of Arimathea. All four Gospels record his single short appearance on the stage of the Passion drama,[1] all say that he was a disciple of Jesus, but the Fourth Gospel alone appends the qualifying phrase, "a secret disciple for fear of the Jews".[2] We have fixed on that phrase, as though it tells the whole story of Joseph, as though the supreme fact about him were not his loyalty to Christ but his fear of making that loyalty known. Intentionally or not, we have pictured him as a coward.

Many writers have portrayed him in that unfavourable light. One, whom I know personally and respect highly, describes Joseph as the only unhappy man among Jesus' followers on Easter Day[3] It was the unhappiness of a man who had supported Jesus but not with a whole-hearted support, the unhappiness of a man who discovers to his sorrow that a tiny bunch of flowers to the living is worth a dozen wreaths to the dead. This writer suggests that Joseph, as a member of the Jewish Council, might have done something to stop the crucifixion of Jesus, but he wasn't even present at the meeting that condemned Jesus to be worthy of death. Perhaps he intended to go, but it was late at night, and his wife may have said, "Don't go, Joseph, it will only make your cold worse." On Easter Day he could not celebrate the victory because he had not fought in the battle. That's what we might conclude, if the single qualifying phrase in John's Gospel were all that we know about Joseph of Arimathea.

The truth is that we know a great deal more. Though he appears only once in the drama, and though each Gospel writer gives him no more than five verses containing only a few pertinent facts, yet when we add up those facts and put them all together we have a surprisingly complete picture. We know, for example, that Joseph came from the Judean town of Arimathea which is not marked on any map, ancient or modern, but which must have been in the vicinity of Jerusalem, else why would he have his private burial garden in Jerusalem? We know that he was a man of means, a landowner or a merchant or the recipient of inherited wealth. We are told he was "a good and upright man" — an epitaph that many of us would like to have on our tombstones. He looked forward to the kingdom of God — which indicates that he was a devoutly religious man who believed in the final triumph of God's purpose. He was a member of the Council, probably a Pharisee, one of the religious aristocracy, a decision-maker in the affairs of the Jewish nation. He was a disciple of Jesus — not just an admirer or even a follower from afar but a disciple who lived close to his Lord and learned from him and was probably the only member of the Sanhedrin to stand up for him. The Gospel explicitly says that "he had dissented from their policy and the action they had taken".

Those are the facts about Joseph before his appearance in the Passion drama. What did he do when he actually came on stage? The Gospel says that just before sundown on Good Friday he bravely went to Pontius Pilate and asked for the body of Jesus. That took bravery, because it identified him with a lost cause and because the Roman Governor was probably still in a foul temper after being humiliated at the trial of Jesus. We don't know whether money changed hands, as it often did on those occasions, but we do know that for some reason Pilate granted the request. We know that Joseph's courage influenced Nicodemus, another Pharisee who once defended Jesus in the Council [4] and who had a remarkable interview with Jesus one night. [5] The two men went to Calvary and removed the mangled corpse from the cross. Accompanied by some of the women, they carried their precious burden to Joseph's own garden located not far from the place of crucifixion. At one end of it, cut into the rock face, was an unused tomb which he had prepared as his own private burial chamber. In that tomb they buried the body of Jesus.

We know the kind of man that Joseph was. We know what he did on Good Friday. Putting all those factors together, do they add up to the picture of a cowardly disciple who was in any way inferior to the other disciples — to Judas who betrayed Jesus,[6] Peter who denied him,[7] Thomas who doubted him,[8] and all the others who deserted him?[9] On the contrary, they show us a man of courage, the only man not afraid to come into the daylight when all the others lurked in the shadows, a man who rose to the occasion and gave Jesus the service that he most needed. What more could any man do than Joseph did?

Our Debt to Joseph

Sir William Osler, the great teacher and practitioner of medicine, a man of deep sympathy and generosity, once performed a service that reflected the character of Joseph of Arimathea. It happened during the 1875 smallpox epidemic in Montreal. At that time Osler was a professor at McGill University. In his club one day he noticed a young Englishman who seemed desperately ill and he advised him to go right home to bed. He called in a specialist who diagnosed the case as malignant smallpox. Osler arranged for the patient's immediate transfer to an isolation hospital and had him placed in a private ward. Next day he went to see him and found him fully aware of his dangerous condition. The young man was dying and he knew it. He spoke of his home and his mother and asked Osler to read the 43rd chapter of Isaiah which his mother had marked in his Bible. Osler stayed beside him until midnight. The young man had no one else in Canada. He was a stranger in a strange land. Toward the end he recited some prayers. Suddenly he grasped the doctor's hand and said quite plainly, "Oh, thanks." Then he died. It is all described in the sympathetic letter that Osler wrote to the boy's parents in England. You can imagine their inexpressible gratitude to this kindly physician.[10]

Christians have felt the same gratitude toward Joseph of Arimathea. We don't have to speculate what would have happened if he had not gone to Pilate and claimed the body of Jesus and buried it in his own private sepulchre. It would not have been buried even in a pauper's grave. Like the bodies of all criminals it would have been thrown into the valley of Gehenna and burned. The other friends of Jesus made no move to prevent that. They couldn't prevent it. They were all in hiding somewhere. Only Joseph, accompanied by Nicodemus and a few women, came forward to perform the last tender and sacred offices of love and respect. He was the undertaker, the officiant and the chief mourner. He gave the body of Jesus a decent, loving, costly burial; and for nineteen centuries Christians have been grateful to him.

Try to imagine the scene in the Passion drama. It is the late afternoon of Good Friday, fast approaching sundown, the beginning of the Jewish Sabbath. We find the hill of Calvary deserted. The brutal show is over, the audience has dispersed, there is nothing more to see. In the stillness after the storm five soldiers guard the crosses, and near them stands a small group of women sobbing silently. Joseph and Nicodemus approach the scene. They speak words of comfort to the women, especially to Mary the mother of Jesus who has returned to be with her son in his death. They show their permit to the centurion who displays a strange interest in what they are about to do. Almost reverently he removes the nails from the hands and feet of Jesus and helps to take the body down from the cross. For a moment Mary holds the lifeless head in her lap and wipes away the blood and the dirt. Gently and tenderly the men lift the limp form and place it on a litter. Followed by the women they move in a sorrowful procession down the hill to a nearby garden of exquisite beauty. In a cool grotto at the end of the garden they lay the body on a bare slab of rock, cleanse and anoint it with costly ointments and enfold it in a linen cloth of delicate texture and fragrance. They look lovingly at it for the last time, then step outside and watch the soldiers as they roll a great cartwheel stone across the mouth of the tomb. Above them the skull-shaped hill and the three emptty crosses stand silhouetted against the darkening sky.

In Jerusalem today you come to a steep cliff shaped like a human skull with a deep trench at the bottom into which it is said that the bodies of victims were thrown after they had been crucified. Not far away is a lovely garden enclosed by a wall that recalls the Gospel verse, "Now at the place where he had been crucified there was a garden." Carved into the sheer rock at one end of the garden is a burial chamber the size of a small room. At the base of the narrow entrance you can see the groove for the cartwheel stone. The curator, an Arab woman of radiant faith, takes you inside and shows you a shelf of rock that looks like a bed and says, "There is the place where they laid him".[11] For Christian pilgrims that garden tomb is one of the most sacred sites in the Holy Land. They find it a moving experience to worship and receive Holy Communion in that place of the risen presence. They find it moving also to sit beneath the trees and among the flowers and simply meditate. Perhaps they think of Joseph of Arimathea, who owned the garden and the tomb and placed them at the disposal of his Lord, and they feel a deep sense of gratitude for the kindness, the generosity and the courage of this little-known man. How deeply indebted we are to Joseph! He buried the body of our Lord. That was the service that he could give.

The Service You can Give

Actually Joseph gave three things to Jesus, and they are the very things that Christians don't give often enough. First, he gave *his influence*. Only a man of influence would have dared to enter the presence of Pontius Pilate and request the body of the man whom the Roman Governor had reluctantly sentenced to death. Only a man of influence could have secured an audience with Pilate. Not one of the disciples, not all of them together, could boast that kind of influence. Joseph, however, was an important man who knew how to deal with important people; he had an entrée to the places of power. He could cut through red tape and pull strings and set

the wheels of political machinery in motion. That was the
service that he could give.

Perhaps too much has been made of Christianity's humble
origins. It is true, as Paul reminded the Corinthians, that few
of the first Christians were "men of wisdom, by any human
standard; few were powerful or highly born".[12]   It is true that
the early Church was built on the labours and loyalty of
ordinary people — farmers, fishermen, shepherds, carpenters
and slaves. But it is true also, and very clear from the New
Testament, that here and there the early Christian communi-
ties included persons of influence who were able to open
doors of opportunity and remove obstacles that impeded the
advancement of the Gospel. When Paul arrived in Philippi
and thereby introduced the Gospel to the continent of
Europe, his first convert was an influential business woman
named Lydia whose home became the centre of the Christian
enterprise in that city.[13] Paul himself was a man of influence,
which is one reason that Christ claimed and converted him
on the Damascus road.[14]   Only such a man could have
quenched the fires of persecution, even momentarily; only
such a man could have moved freely among Gentile cultures;
only such a man could have interpreted the Gospel for his
own and future generations. That was the service that Paul
could give.

Christ needs his humble servants, for in his sight all men
are equally precious and important. Yet there are times when
one man of influence can do more for Christ than a whole
army of humble folk, especially if he is a decision-maker in
politics, business, labour, culture or communications. Think
what it means when a statesman, an elected representative of
the people, a man whose voice carries weight in the councils
of the nation, makes it the main purpose of his life to serve
Jesus Christ. William Wilberforce was such a man. He
started out as a typical eighteenth-century English aristocrat,
elegant, witty and content with the world as he found it. His
deep religious experience destroyed none of his wit and
charm but gave him a new purpose to serve Christ in public
affairs that earned for him the title, "Keeper of the nation's
conscience". Only such a man of influence could have
spearheaded the struggle in the British Parliament that

turned the nation's economy upside down and ended in the abolition of the slave trade. That was the service he could give.

Joseph of Arimathea gave *his wealth* to Jesus. He may not have given all his wealth, such as Jesus required from the Rich Young Ruler,[15] but he gave more than any of the other disciples, perhaps all of them together, were able to give. We assume that he had to buy the body of Jesus from Pontius Pilate; and it has been suggested that the asking price was thirty pieces of silver — a substantial and significant sum, though Pilate may not have grasped its significance. Who else among the followers of Jesus had the means to handle the situation on Good Friday? Who else had an unused tomb ready and waiting for the body of his Lord? Who else possessed a private burial garden of such exquisite beauty? Who else, after the curtain had fallen on the tragic drama of the Crucifixion, could have stepped into the footlights and given Jesus the service that Joseph gave?

It is one of the anomalies of Christianity that, while exalting poverty as a virtue, its work has been continually advanced by its wealthy benefactors. Again too much has been made of the window's mite syndrome, as though Christ cared not about the size of a man's gift but only about the amount of money he has left in his pocket. If that were true, a great many Christian enterprises would have gone bankrupt or would never have been started in the first place. Think of the Christian colleges and seminaries at home and abroad that exercise a uniquely influential ministry through the total immersion of generations of young people in an atmosphere of Christian principles and learning. In most cases they owe their existence and survival to the gifts and endowments of their benefactors. Many of their buildings bear the names of the donors. One who refused to have his name publicised said, "I don't want to be thanked. It's something I can do, a service that I can give."

No company of Christians works more effectively and sacrificially among poor people than does the Salvation Army. Salvationists themselves have few financial resources. Where do they find the money for their hospitals, youth hostels, training colleges and redemptive homes? They receive it from generous benefactors who appreciate the work that they are doing and feel privileged to share in that work through their financial gifts. There was a man who arranged his investments so that a substantial capital sum would be available to the Salvation Army if he lived beyond a certain date. He explained the situation to a pair of officers who came to see him about the projects for which the money would be used. One of them said, "You mean that your only problem is that you must live for another six months? That can be taken care of very simply. Let us pray..."

Joseph of Arimathea gave *his reputation*. He may have kept his discipleship secret before the Crucifixion, but the word was out once the soldiers and priests saw the body of Jesus being carried down the hill and through the gate of Joseph's private garden. You can just hear the buzzing in the Sanhedrin: "That traitor Joseph! No wonder he dissented from our policy and action. He's one of them. He has been one of them all the time. He should be arrested!" Do you think that Joseph was able to take his seat in the Council after that? It is more likely that he was expelled from the Council and, perhaps, from the synagogue which, as we saw in the case of the man born blind, was the severest penalty that could be inflicted on any first-century Jew. Joseph laid his reputation on the line when he officiated at the funeral of Jesus.

Many people have given that same service to Christ. They have stood for him or for one of his principles or for some part of his teaching, knowing that they would not be popular for it but might even be called scoundrels and fools. So it was with Martin Luther who pitted himself against the hierarchy of a corrupt Church and refused to recant, saying, "Here I stand. I cannot do otherwise. God help me!" So it must have been with Albert Schweitzer when he first announced that he intended to relinquish his secure and lucrative careers in music and theology and qualify as a general practitioner of medicine to serve as a missionary in French Equatorial Africa. People must have said, "You will be a nobody there"; but for the sake of Christ he was willing to be a nobody, willing to lay his reputation on the line. That was the service he could give.

It may be the service you can give. It is the service that you *must* give once you have seen the Cross. Whether or not Joseph was a secret disciple before Good Friday, it is certain that, once he saw his Lord nailed to that wooden gallows, he could keep his secret no longer. From the Cross came both the challenge and the courage to serve Jesus openly and publicly no matter what it cost him. There is an ancient superstition that a man cannot safely die until he has taken a stick and marked the earth with the sign of a cross. Superstition or not, it contains a profoundly important truth — that somewhere on earth our lives ought to make the sign of a cross, else we shall not safely live or safely die. Ultimately every Christian must take the principle of the Cross, the principle of love and sacrifice, to the centre of his life. That is the service he can give, the service you can give.

CHAPTER NOTES:

1. Mark 15:42-47;
   Matt. 27:557-61
   Luke 23:50-54
   John 19:38-42
2. John 19:38
3. Leslie D. Weatherhead,
   Personalities of the Passion
   (Hodder and Stoughton Ltd.,
   1942) p. 122ff.
4. John 7:50-52
5. John 3:1ff.
6. Matt. 26:14-16
7. Mark 14:66-72
8. John 20:19-29
9. Mark 14:50
10. Edith Gittings Reid,
    The Great Physician
    (Oxford University Press,
    London, 1947) pp. 48-49
11. Mark 16:6
12. 1 Cor. 1:26
13. Acts 17:11-15
14. Acts 9:1ff.
15. Mark 10:17-22

20
Mary Magdelene

Fiction and Facts

MARY MAGDELENE IS one of the most fascinating, mysterious, elusive, yet clearly portrayed women in the New Testament. "Magdalene" simply denotes that she came from Magdala, a village between Tiberius and Capernaum on the western shore of the Sea of Galilee. You can visit its ruins today. Mary appears in all four Gospels. She is a real person in the drama, a true supporting character of Jesus. She must not be confused with the other Marys of whom there are six in the New Testament, just as there are several men with the name of John.

We sometimes confuse Mary Magdalene with Mary of Bethany, the sister of Martha and Lazarus, who sat at Jesus' feet and drank in his heavenly words when she might have been helping her sister with the housework.[1] Mary Magdalene has also been confused with the woman of loose moral character who crashed a dinner part and anointed the feet of Jesus with costly ointment, much to the disgust of the guests.[2] She has even been identified with the woman taken in adultery whose accusers Jesus condemned when he said, "He that is without sin among you, let him first cast a stone at her."[3] One writer puts all those women into a melting pot, and out comes Mary Magdalene. Her seven devils were seven husbands, of whom one left her a jar of costly ointment. She meets Jesus in Jericho and receives his forgiveness for her sins. At Bethany she anoints his feet with the ointment and is later caught in an act of adultery and again forgiven by Jesus.[4] That rather comprehensive arrangement taxes the imagination.

Another favourite fallacy about Mary Magdalene is that she was in love with Jesus and was even his mistress, at least in a spiritual sense. That comes across from the motion picture version of *Jesus Christ Superstar* [5] and it is the one feature that really offends our Christian sensibilities. We listen to her famous song which contains the line, "I've had so many men before"; yet there is nothing in the New Testament to suggest that Mary had any men before or after she met Jesus. Why do playwrights and novelists nearly always portray her as a prostitute? Does the Gospel record yield one shred of evidence to support that low estimate of her character?

We know exactly five things about Mary apart from the fact that she came from Magdala: (1) She was cured of demon-possession by Jesus. (2) She became one of a group of women disciples of Jesus. (3) She was at the Cross on Good Friday. (4) She helped to bury the body of Jesus. (5) She was the first person to see Jesus alive after his Resurrection. Those facts do not identify Mary as a prostitute but they do identify her as an important character in the Gospel drama, a real person with a very definite spiritual history. We could call that spiritual history "The Whole Easter Experience".

Made Whole Again

It began when Jesus moved into her life with an act of Divine grace and power. Mary had been insane, possessed by seven devils, so people said. Much of the time she was a normal young woman, but sometimes all hell broke loose within her. She screamed, cursed, writhed and had to be forcibly restrained lest she injure herself and others. It must have been a terrible burden for her parents. We can imagine them talking in a mood of despair. They can hear Mary singing in the next room. Her father says, "Listen to her. The devils are not tormenting her now. Who would dream that such madness could come upon her at times? Would to God that there was a way of helping her!"

"There is a way, husband," his wife says eagerly.

"Do not torment me, wife. Have we not tried everything? Have we not consulted the physicians? Have we not prayed?

Have we not offered temple sacrifices? There is no way of helping her."

"There is, husband. Jesus of Nazareth…"

"That mad carpenter! That charlatan! Are you crazy, wife?"

"But he's not mad. He's not a charlatan. He heals people. Susanna was telling me only yesterday what he did for Joseph's boy. You remember him. He was possessed with devils like our Mary. Jesus healed him. The boy is in his right mind now."

"I don't believe it. And let me tell you, wife. No more talk of this Jesus person. He has a bad reputation. I hear that the authorities are planning to arrest him."

"Well it doesn't matter. I've asked him to come here."

"You've what?"

"I've asked him to come here. Oh husband, what does it matter what the authorities think of him? How many of them know what it is to see your only child torn to pieces by seven devils? We can't afford to be proud. Our daughter must be healed, and I have faith that Jesus can do it."

They are interrupted by a servant who seems rather flustered. "Mistress, there's a group of men outside. One of them is…Jesus of Nazareth. He says that you sent for him."

"Yes, yes, show them inside. Stay, husband. Jesus may succeed where others have failed."

Three men enter the room. Two of them are rough and weather-beaten, like fishermen. The third also has the physique of a labourer but the face of an artist or a saint. His piercing gaze rests upon the father who tries to turn away. Then he looks at the mother and asks, "Where is your daughter?"

Slowly, almost fearfully she opens a door and calls, "Mary."

A girl comes through the open door. She is demure and pretty but painfully shy. At the sight of Jesus the half-smile vanishes from her face which becomes contorted, and she screams in the voice of a man, "Leave me alone…Jesus of Nazareth…Leave me alone…Son of God…do not torment me…"

"Come out of her, you unclean spirit!"

There is shocked silence. What is this voice of authority? It is like the voice of God. Mary stands as if petrified, then sinks to the floor. Her parents move toward her.

"Leave her alone," says Jesus.

Gradually her convulsive breathing becomes quieter. She could almost be sleeping. Her eyes open. They look clear, normal and sane. Mary smiles at her parents, then looks at Jesus and sees the sympathy and tenderness in his face. She rises to her feet, slowly approaches him, kneels down and kisses the hem of his garment. Placing his hand upon her head, Jesus calls her by name, "Mary."

"My Master," she replies.

That's how it might have started — the spiritual history of Mary Magdalene. It began when Jesus moved into her life with an act of Divine grace and power and did for her what no one else could do and what she could not do for herself. That's where every Christian's spiritual history begins, because that's where the Gospel begins — with God taking the initiative and moving into our human situation with an act of Divine grace and power. The Gospel does not begin with man erecting a ladder of reasoned argument or mystic contemplation or moral achievement and trying to climb from earth to heaven. It begins with God letting down a ladder and coming where we are, entering our lives, casting out our devils and restoring us to health and wholeness of personality. That is the first step in the whole Easter experience.

Sharing Christ's Ministry

As a second step Mary became one of a group of women disciples who followed Jesus and shared his ministry. Apparently they all came out of a similar experience. Luke writes about them, and that is typical of Luke who was a Gentile and therefore not inhibited by Jewish male prejudice. In his account of Jesus' ministry he includes this paragraph:

After this he went journeying from town to town and village to village, proclaiming the good news of the kingdom of God. With him were the Twelve and a number of women who had been set free from evil spirits and infirmities: Mary, known as Mary of Magdala, from whom seven devils had come out, Joanna, the wife of Chuza a steward of Herod's, Susanna, and many others. These women provided for them out of their own resources.[6]

That fixes the place of women in the earliest days of Christianity and dispels any illusions that they were second-class Christians. Along with the other disciples they proclaimed the kingdom of God, they provided material assistance, they supported and shared the Gospel ministry of Jesus. That was their response to all that Jesus had done for them. Their service was an expression of love and gratitude — which is the only valid motive, the only working dynamic of Christian service. One reason why Christians so often weaken in their commitment to Christ, one reason why they cease to serve him and fall away from his Church is that they get the proper sequence reversed. They try to take the second step in the Easter experience without having taken the first step. They try to do great things for God without ever having allowed God to do great things for them.

On the other hand, the whole Easter experience is arrested unless the Christian, having been helped by Christ, then joins the company of those who consciously share the ministry of Christ. It is a priestly ministry that brings God and man together, reconciling men to God and therefore to one another. It is a saving ministry that reaches into the dark places of life and rescues people from degradation, doubt and despair. It is a teaching ministry that proclaims in word and action the truth of God's love and purpose and power. It is a healing ministry that comforts the broken-hearted and binds up their wounds and restores them to health of body and mind. It is a serving ministry that feeds the hungry and clothes the naked and shelters the homeless and works for the redemption of all society. "We have this ministry,"[7] wrote Paul, the ministry of Christ which he began on earth and continues through his living presence; and to exercise that ministry and share it with Christ is the second step in the whole Easter experience.

Beneath the Cross

The next thing that we know about Mary Magdalene is that she was at the Cross. She could answer "Yes" to the question, "Were you there when they crucified my Lord?" All the Gospel writers find her at Calvary, standing at a distance from the Cross in a tiny group of women who had followed Jesus and waited on him when he was in Galilee.[8] They look like lambs in a lair of lions. Did the crucifiers of Jesus turn their anger on them? "You, Mary of Magdala, go home to Galilee where you belong, instead of disgracing yourself like this."

"Yes, Mary of Magdala", thunders a priest. "Your sins are many for following this blasphemer."

Two Roman soldiers approach the women. Having drunk deeply of the pre-crucifixion wine issue, they walk unsteadily and talk in slurred voices. One of them sees Mary. "Well, well, what have we got here? Look, Fluvius, here's a pretty piece. Send the others home, but she can stay."

The tall centurion who commands the execution detail catches sight of the little party. His face wears a strange expression. The whole experience is affecting him visibly. He orders the soldiers away and speaks gently to the women, "You are followers of the Nazarene? This is no place for you. I'll give you a bodyguard and get you out of here."

Mary pleads, "Oh no, sir. Please let us stay. We are his friends. This is his mother. Please don't ask us to leave. We are all that he has left."

"As you wish, then. But you, young woman, you had better go. You are not safe here. These men..."

Mary is weeping now. "I can't leave him", she pleads. "He gave me my life."

For every Christian the Easter experience goes by way of a cross. Indeed, there can be no crown without a cross, no resurrection that does not follow a crucifixion, no victory that does not rise out of defeat. That was supremely true for Jesus himself who, as Paul writes, "humbled himself and became obedient unto death, even death on a cross". "Therefore," declares Paul — the key word is *therefore* — "God has highly exalted him and bestowed on him the name which is above every name..."[9] The Resurrection was God's verdict on his Son's perfect obedience. There can be no path to glory that does not go by way of a cross.

Among the hotels in the famous Roman Catholic shrine at Lourdes in France there is one called "Gethsemane", advertised as a desirable stopping-place "with all modern comforts". That typical anomaly may explain why for so many people the sense of glory, hope and expectation has departed from the Christian life. They have not paid the price for it. They have nothing to look forward *to* because they have nothing to look forward *from*. They are like soldiers who cannot celebrate a victory because they did not fight in the battle. During the Boxer rebellion in China a missionary was stoned by the very people whom he had loved and served. When he felt the warm blood trickling down his face he said, "At last I am a Christian." No martyr complex there; only the awareness that the way of Jesus leads to a cross, that sharing the ministry of Christ means sharing the sufferings of Christ. The Cross is a principle at the heart of the Christian life, a principle of obedience, sacrifice, suffering and death that no follower of Christ can escape of should want to escape. It is an essential step in the whole Easter experience.

Faithful to the End

The next thing we know about Mary Magdalene is that she helped to bury the body of Jesus. She stayed to the end, she and one other nameless woman. None of the disciples was there. We can be sure that only John of all the apostles witnessed any part of the Crucifixion. Even he, at a command from the Cross, took Mary the mother of Jesus away.[10] Jesus dismissed his mother but he did not dismiss Mary Magdalene. She would not be dismissed. She watched the conclusion of the dreadful drama, heard the cry of dereliction in the darkness,[11] listened to her Lord shout, "It is accomplished,"[12] and commit his soul to God,[13] then saw his head drop in death. The crowds in their panic dispersed,[14] but Mary stayed there and drew closer to the Cross in spite of the leering gaze of the soldiers. When Joseph of Arimathea and Nicodemus arrived, she helped to take the bloodstained corpse down from the Cross, she washed the body of Jesus with her tears and dried it with her hair, she followed the mournful procession to the tomb in Joseph's garden and stood there sorrowfully as the soldiers sealed it with a great stone.[15] Of all the followers of Jesus Mary alone stayed to the very end.

That is the longest and loneliest step in the whole Easter experience, and not many Christians are prepared to take it. You take it when your loyalty to Christ brings you to a point where others have fallen away from him and you alone share his final defeat and agony and humiliation at the Cross. Yet Mary is not really alone. Beside her and around her stands a great unseen company that includes saints, reformers, confessors and martyrs of all the centuries who not only gave their loyalty to Christ but stayed with him to the end. They include Archbishop Berggrav of Norway who asked the Nazis, when they threatened to shoot him for his Christian witness, "And what will you do to me after that?" They include the daughter of a Chinese pastor who, when the persecution of the Church was at its worst in the 1950s, wrote to her parents outside China, "Do not try to contact me. We are walking the road from Gethsemane to Calvary." They include little pockets of the faithful in western democracies who, when their contemporaries have been dazzled by the illusions of the secular culture, still profess their faith in God and still remain loyal to Christ and his Church. They have taken an essential step in the whole Eastern experience.

The Easter Experience

The great thing that we know about Mary is that she was an eye-witness of the Resurrection, in fact the first person on this earth to see the Risen Christ alive. The Gospels are unanimous on that fact. They differ in some details but they all give first place to Mary. Matthew begins his account of the Resurrection, "The Sabbath had passed, and it was about daybreak on Sunday when Mary of Magdala and the other Mary came to look at the grave..."[16] Mark begins, "When the Sabbath was over, Mary of Magdala, Mary the Mother of

James, and Salome, brought aromatic oils intending to go and anoint him..."[17] Later he says about Jesus, "When he had risen from the dead early on Sunday morning he appeared first to Mary of Magdala, from whom he had formerly cast out seven devils..."[18]

John's account moves us most deeply.[19] Mary comes to the tomb by herself early on Sunday morning even before dawn. Presumably she intends to anoint the body of her Lord with perfumes and spices. It will not bring him back but at least it will express her undying devotion to him. As she steps through the gate into the quiet garden, it seems that her eyes are playing tricks on her. In the half-light she sees the stone not standing against the mouth of the tomb but lying on the ground some distance away. She rushes back into the city to find Peter and John and tell them that someone has stolen the body of Jesus. The two men race to the garden and come to the tomb. When John, after pausing reverently on the threshold, steps inside and sees the grave clothes undisturbed, he knows immediately what has happened. Then Mary enters and sees a vision of angels to whom she pours out her lament, "They have taken my Lord away, and I do not know where they have laid him". As she steps outside and stands there sobbing silently, another voice arouses her. "Why are you weeping? What is it you are looking for?" Through her tears she can make out a figure standing beside her. Thinking him to be the gardener, she pleads, "If it is you, sir, who removed him, tell me where you have laid him, and I will take him away". Then she hears her name, "Mary", as only one person on earth can speak that name. Two years fall away. She is in her father's home looking into the face of the one who gave her life. Now she looks into that face again and cries with glad recognition, "My Master!"

Mary Magdalene! The first eye-witness of the Resurrection! The first person on earth to whom the Risen Christ appeared alive! Why Mary? Why this unimportant woman from Magdala? Why not John, the beloved disciple, or Peter or one of the other apostles? We can only conclude that there must have been something special about Mary, something that made her more spiritually qualified than the other followers of Jesus, something that prepared her to encounter and recognize the Risen Christ. We can only conclude that the Resurrection came to her, not as an isolated event but as the inevitable climax of a total spiritual experience.

It is only as the climax of a total experience that the event of Easter makes any sense to anybody. If Easter doesn't turn you on, if it doesn't seem important to you or even credible, if you don't want to leap in the air and wave your arms and shout hallelujahs, if you don't really believe or care that Christ rose from the dead — don't blame the Bible or the Church or the theologians. Look for the fault in yourself. Perhaps you are not spiritually qualified to celebrate Easter. You may need to begin further back — with the grace of God that Christ brings into your life, with the service that you can give to Christ in the sharing of his ministry, with your fellowship in his sufferings and your loyalty to the very end. Then you might believe the Resurrection. You might even see the Risen Christ. Then you will have the whole Easter experience.

CHAPTER NOTES:

1. Luke 10:38-42
2. Mark 14:3-9; Matt. 26:6-13; Luke 7:36-50; John 12:1-8
3. John 8:1-11 (K.J.V.)
4. Edwin McNeill Poteat, *These Shared His Power* (Harper and Brothers, New York, 1948) p. 29ff.
5. Op. cit.
6. Luke 8:1-3
7. 2 Cor. 4:1
8. Mark 15:40-41; Matt. 27:55-56 John 19:25-26
9. Phil. 2:8-9 (R.S.V.)
10. John 19:26-27
11. Matt. 27:45-46
12. John 19:30
13. Luke 24:46
14. Luke 23:48
15. Mark 15:42-47; Matt. 27:57-61
16. Matt. 28:1
17. Mark 16:1
18. Mark 16:9
19. John 20:1-18